Using Picture Books to Teach Comprehension Strategies

Joanne M. Zimny

SCHOLASTIC

New York • Toronto • London • Auckland • Sydney
Mexico City • New Delhi • Hong Kong • Buenos Aires

Dedication

For Jim Zimny,

the love of my life and the strongest man I know

And to our four little blessings,

Daniel James, Mary Agnes, Benjamin Shamus, and Julia Faith.

You guys are the most incredible people in the world.

Cover design by Jason Robinson
Cover photography by Jason Robinson
Interior design by Teresa Southwell
Interior photographs courtesy of the author

ISBN-13: 978-0-545-05399-0
ISBN-10: 0-545-05399-4

Table of Contents

Acknowledgments

Many thanks to my colleagues who contributed their favorite creative ideas to this book, and particularly my editor, Sarah Longhi, who patiently told me how to write a book proposal. Special thanks to librarian extraordinaire Elizabeth A. Roberts for sharing her passion for literacy, and Literacy Coordinator Valerie Bush, aka Central Kitsap's "Superwoman," who has tirelessly gathered strategy instruction lessons for our school district, many of which are shared in this book. She also assisted me in compiling the book lists found at the end of each chapter.

To Amee Coulter, a fellow teacher in the trenches and dear friend, who is always there on the other end of the line saying, "What do you need, Chickie?" You took the book into Alaska and gave me the confidence to push it forward. Thanks for being "911-AMEE" and making me laugh when I really needed it. You are inspiring.

To my darling baby sisters, Nancy and Sandra, who sat through endless hours of my "teaching school" when we were younger. Nancy, I still feel guilty about making you write that ten-page report on the bubonic plague, but you *did* steal my bathing suit. And to my cousin, Anne Wood, who will forever be my kindred spirit in life's journeys.

The deepest appreciation goes to my loving father, Daniel Morris, for being the most animated storyteller in the world. You taught me all I know. And to my beautiful mother, Mary Jean, who continues to do my laundry and hold my hand in parking lots. You both are at the very center of my heart.

Introduction

At the tender age of 21, I had been assigned to my first teaching job in a local fourth-grade class. But by the second month of teaching, my well of ideas had gone dry. My classroom wasn't exactly the exciting place I imagined it would be, particularly when it came to reading and writing. Every morning my students and I would get out our anthology, and we would read stories together. Then I would ask them to start answering the questions. Out came the notebook paper and students grudgingly began their task while I strolled around the silent room making sure everyone was on the right page.

One day, I stopped at the desk of one of my students. His motivation to work diligently increased with me standing nearby. "Josh," I asked quietly, "what'd you think of the character named Laura in the story?"

Josh's head jerked up as soon as he heard his name. "Huh?"

I repeated the question and he shrugged. "I don't know. Is that one of the questions?" He looked down to search page 491.

"No," I answered. "I was just wondering what you thought."

"I wasn't thinking," he explained. "I was just reading it."

The truth hurt. Reading had simply become a to-do list in my classroom. Read together. Answer questions. Turn work in after making sure names are on papers. An alarming realization dawned on me: My students were bored. Every day was the same. We approached every story in the same way. Excitement and joy for reading had evaporated, and it was only October.

That night I headed for the bookstore and stood among the shelves, completely frustrated. I had no idea how to change my teaching, but I knew change had to happen. As I moped about, I spotted a picture book on display. Immediately curious about the book, I walked over and picked it up. I began to read it and was soon drawn into an African folk tale about two sisters with completely different personalities and fates. The gorgeous illustrations depicted the jungles of Nigeria. Plants, birds, and colorful villages and clothing filled each page. I bought *Mufaro's Beautiful Daughters* by John Steptoe and took it to my class the following day.

I called my students to the front of the class and we all sat on the floor together. They sat right next to my knees, and suddenly I felt much more connected. I smiled when I thought how strange some of our teaching practices are, like trying to read to children when they are on the other side of a large classroom. Sharing a book requires proximity to the reader, not chasms. By sitting close by me, I hoped that students would see reading as a sharing process where conversation begins naturally, and the discussion becomes important to everyone.

Mufaro's Beautiful Daughters enthralled my fourth graders. We talked about characters, illustrations, the cultures of Africa, and story organization. We made posters that depicted characters' motives and personalities, gluing student work on a large piece of butcher paper to share. Time lines hung across the ceiling displaying the events of plot, and students made personal connections by writing stories about their own families. We discussed why John Steptoe might have written the book for kids and recorded the reasons on sticky notes and posted them on the board. I noticed some of students made "booklets" to record and reflect on discussions. They had time to share thoughts with the rest of the class and ask their own questions about the story and its meaning.

By the end of the day the walls of the classroom had been transformed, but more important, I had changed how I thought students could learn. By discussion, teamwork, and moving abstract thinking into the concrete realm through writing and pictures, I was allowing time for students to construct meaning for themselves. The rewards were astounding. My classroom hummed like a beehive, comprehension was at an all-time high, and despite all the movement and materials, students remained focused and excited about reading.

But amazingly, I did not introduce another picture book that year. In my profound lack of experience, that day remained isolated and I went right back to teaching the way I had been. I remained stubbornly loyal to my training, because I felt torn about this new way to teach. I saw it as taking too much classroom and planning time, and I still viewed curriculum as being determined by textbooks. Anything I added to the textbook must be just for fun with limited academic benefit. My room seemed "noisy," and I battled with the belief that students should remain seated and quiet for optimal learning, even though in my case I had witnessed quite the opposite. It seemed the upper elementary grades had abandoned reading carpets, class gatherings, and picture books. What was I doing, thinking I could use these techniques with older kids?

That was more than twenty years ago. As I increased my training, experience, and knowledge about how children learn, I gradually became more confident in my philosophy and brought it into my daily teaching. I explored reading research, visited highly successful classrooms, talked with colleagues, and read inspiring teaching books. I found much support for active learning in the classroom after all. Where *Mufaro's Beautiful Daughters* once sat alone on a shelf, I have since added hundreds of other picture books. I now see my picture book library as a collection of art—and the heart of my teaching tools.

In my readings I discovered the 1978 landmark work of reading researcher Dolores Durkin, who initiated many changes in the world of reading instruction. After extensive observations of comprehension instruction in classrooms, Durkin noticed that comprehension instruction followed a general format: Teachers would read a text with students and then merely assess comprehension by using teacher-generated questions at the end. The actual teaching of reading strategies, the major component of comprehension instruction, was missing. The strategies of visualizing, questioning text, inferring author purpose, predicting solutions, determining important ideas, and summarizing to foster remembering were rarely modeled or scaffolded during the reading of books.

Almost 30 years after Durkin's work, researcher Michael Pressley made this provocative statement to the International Reading Research Convention in 2006: "What to do? It is time to do some serious research on how to develop teachers who can provide comprehension strategies instruction that does produce students who learn to use and do use these strategies in a self-regulated fashion . . . Such professional development will require developing modeling, explanation, and scaffolding skills in teachers, as well as a commitment to teach and encourage comprehension strategies every day." The need for strategy instruction in the classroom remains a challenge today, despite the years of research supporting its importance. My hope is that this book can help you meet that challenge.

How This Book Works

Each of the six chapters of *Using Picture Books to Teach Comprehension Strategies* provides a mini-unit on a particular reading strategy. Chapters begin with a quick introduction, followed by an introductory modeling lesson to share with students. In this first lesson, I read the picture book aloud, stopping intermittently to talk about the book and think out loud, modeling my thought processes for students. I also make sure I show my emotional involvement with the story, expressing wonder, confusion, joy, sadness, or anger over what is being said in the text to make it clear to students that reading touches us emotionally and provides a window onto the human condition.

I follow the first lesson with *scaffolded* lessons. David Pearson, a prominent reading researcher, describes scaffolding as "what teachers say and do to enable children to complete complex mental tasks they could not complete without assistance" (Pearson & Fielding, 1991). In the scaffolded lessons, I gradually release responsibility for applying the strategy to students. I decrease my thinking aloud and modeling, encouraging students to respond, discuss, and attempt to apply the strategy. It is important that students be able to define the strategy in their own words and have opportunities to apply it with my guidance. As students gain confidence and understanding, we move from whole-class strategy practice to small-group collaboration, and later to individual practice. Scaffolded lessons are extremely valuable because they allow me to check for understanding, listen for misconceptions, and pre-assess student ability.

Assessment and extension lessons or activities are also included for most chapters.

My approach to designing these strategy units is based on the elements of powerful instruction explored in researcher Richard Allington's book *What Really Matters for Struggling Readers: Designing Research Based Programs*, 2005. My goal is to have lessons that progress gradually from teacher demonstration to complex, independent application by students.

Here are descriptions of a few other sections you'll find in the chapters.

Secret Ingredient: Extension ideas for other lessons
Selecting Picture Books: These are questions you can use to find other suitable books to teach the strategy.
Reading Workshop Link: This section provides suggestions for extending new strategies into independent reading. Time for individual practice of strategic reading remains the essential piece in powerful reading instruction. Without it, strategy instruction is like teaching students to swim without ever allowing them in the pool. During reading workshop, my students read free-choice books and document learning in their Reading Journals.

The Joy of Reading

My goal in writing *Using Picture Books to Teach Comprehension Strategies* is to show you a classroom in which strategy instruction strengthens students' reading abilities while fostering enjoyment of books. The strategy lessons presented have been used repeatedly in classrooms because they actively engage students, clearly articulate and define reading strategies, and incorporate high-quality literature.

There is one caution. Reading strategies should not be the end goal. Strategy lessons should be wrapped within a content area or an academic theme and viewed merely as tools to create understanding. When students are asked what they are studying, the answer shouldn't be, "We are learning about determining importance." The answer should be, "We are learning about forest ecosystems by being able to determine what is important in a text."

I hope you will see the following lessons as starting points for your own creativity and that they will invigorate your teaching. I see myself as still learning about our wonderful profession, so these lessons are humbly presented and primarily meant to inspire you. Feel free to use them as catalysts for your own objectives. Bring in your favorite books and themes and adjust the lessons to fit your students' needs. My hope is that you become empowered to develop your own strategy lessons and explore the amazing world of literature with students. May your classroom always be a place of great joy and wonderment as you delve into the art of picture books.

Chapter 1

Visualizing

Lessons at a Glance

Lesson 1 *Color Me a Rhyme:* Pre-Assessing Visualizing Ability
Lesson 2 *This Little Light of Mine:* Introducing the Concept of Visualizing
Lesson 3 *The Midnight Ride of Paul Revere* and *Paul Revere's Ride:* Visualizing Story Events
Lesson 4 *Thirteen Moons on Turtle's Back:* Scaffolding Visualization to Determine Setting

The importance of teaching visualizing always reminds me of a time I was working with a fourth-grade student who was still reading at the primer level. Despite many interventions, Tara's progress remained painstakingly slow. One day after a visualizing lesson, Tara was lining up for lunch. I remember her standing there at the front of the line, holding her brown snack bag. She said to me, "Mrs. Zimny? You know when you were talking about how our brains have a white board, and we can draw on them in our minds?" I nodded, and she waited a few seconds before saying, "Well, I never thought of that before." I was stunned to hear this. In all my years of teaching it never occurred to me that some students do not know how to utilize this vital strategy. They have merely viewed reading as decoding words, an event devoid of meaning. This can definitely change when we work on the visualizing strategy (Harvey & Goudvis, 2007).

Visualizing: A Definition

Visualizing is the configuration of pictures in our minds through sensory experience when we read text (Zimmermann & Keene, 2007). Explanation and purposeful instruction of visualizing become essential to reinforcing this strategy while reading, particularly for students who are challenged in this area. Because each student has different schemas or background knowledge, these images can never be exactly alike. All minds are unique, pulling in personal experiences, individual relationships, and prior concepts to interpret text. Thus, in our teaching we allow individuality, while at the same time reinforcing that universal images exist in text. If the text says the cat is gray, well, that is what we want our students visualize, keeping them as close to the story meaning as possible.

Katerina is drawing about a poem in *Color Me a Rhyme*.

Selecting Picture Books to Support Visualizing Strategy Instruction

Here are some questions to ask as you choose books for strategy lessons on visualizing.

◆ Does the text help the reader create mental images using the five senses?

◆ Is vivid description used to describe the characters and/or setting?

◆ Are there examples of metaphor, simile, and personification to help students recognize these literary devices used to develop imagery?

◆ Do detailed illustrations truly mirror the descriptions and imagery of the text?

◆ With a poetry picture book, does the text contain concrete images?

Literary theorist Peter Rabinowitz (1998) includes the comprehension strategy of visualizing in his landmark book *Before Reading*, a book intended to support graduate-level study of literature. However, I think his concepts most definitely apply to our work as literature teachers at the elementary level. Rabinowitz firmly stated, "We cannot attend to everything equally" as we read. He believed strong readers depended on four "Rules of Notice" that foster deep comprehension of text. Noting striking detail and images in the text comprise the very first rule, and this includes noting imagery to visualize setting, character, and plot to increase comprehension (Serafini, 2004).

It is through the strategy of visualizing that reading takes us into the adventurous realm of books. I treasure the moments when my students can escape from the chaos of life in a classroom and delve into a faraway and foreign land. I can still see Jason, sitting cross-legged in the middle of my active classroom, oblivious to fellow students, completely engrossed in a book about zebras. I knew he had left us for the wide savannas cascading across Africa. Tomorrow, he may be on a Civil War battlefield or lost in a mystical place called Narnia. This is the true wonder and miracle of teaching children to read. I cannot assume that every student practices the strategy of visualizing to improve comprehension. For some, like Tara, it may have never occurred to them that this can be the whole point of reading for pleasure. It is important that the teaching of this strategy begin with lots of teacher modeling and scaffolding of student effort. (Note: To find more lessons and ideas regarding The Rules of Notice, see lesson 3.4 in Frank Serafini's 2004 book, *Lessons in Comprehension*.)

Lesson 1:
Pre-Assessing Visualizing Ability

Color Me a Rhyme
Author: Jane Yolen
Photographer: Jason Semple
Boyds Mills Press

Learning objective:
Students will illustrate a poem accurately using details from the text.

Posting work provides examples for students and also documents learning over time.

Anything by Jane Yolen is perfect for visualizing. She is a master of descriptive language, and her little poetry book titled *Color Me a Rhyme* provides a great starting place. The poems are simple and brief, making them perfect for pre-assessing students. Also, photographer Jason Semple, who happens to be Yolen's son, provides phenomenal nature pictures focused on specific color poems. Different pages devoted to assorted colors make this book fun. On each page Yolen also includes lists of alternative color words, which are terrific to chart and leave up for later writing workshops.

Materials

Color Me a Rhyme
Large butcher paper with copy of book cover
    glued to center
4 or 5 copies each of Yolen's poems
Colored pencils
8 x 8-inch squares of white construction
    paper (one for each student)

One team's interpretation of the poem "Blue."

What to Do

1. Gather students on the carpet so they are sitting close to you.

2. Introduce Yolen's book and explain her relationship to the photographer.

3. Read some poems, without showing the photographs.

4. Give each student a copy of a different color poem. ("White," "Black," "Scarlet," "Pink: A Haiku," "Gray," and "Brown" work the best.)

After sharing some of the poems, invite students to choose a color poem to illustrate individually. I usually make four or five copies of six color poems. Students choose a poem and then illustrate what they think that page in the book must look like. I ask them: What subject in nature do you think Jason Semple photographed to support the descriptive language in the poem?

5. Ask them to read the poems quietly and draw what they see. I remind students to keep their pictures top secret from their peers.

6. Come back to the carpet and allow students to post their pictures on the butcher paper.

When we gather on the carpet again, I have butcher paper hanging nearby with a photocopy of each poem already pasted up. Students attach their illustrations near their posted poem and we discuss. Point out how the pictures may be different or the same.

7. Read Yolen's book again and share the pictures.

As we reread the book, we discuss how our pictures are different or similar from Semple's. I like to emphasize the word *schema* at this point and talk about how everyone has different "movies" in their brain based on their own personal experiences.

8. Assess each child's performance by checking the accuracy and detail of his or her drawing.

As a teacher, I find activities such as this one intriguing. This simple activity shows so much about a child's ability to visualize. I note how my strong readers can depict the essence of their poems with great detail. Challenged readers tend to draw pictures that lack substance and include no real information from the poem itself. As I mentioned earlier, I had assumed that all students utilized the strategy of visualizing, but now know this isn't true. I am always in search of picture books with beautiful language and unusual descriptions that will foster the creation of images within the minds of my students.

Secret Ingredient: This lesson can be used with any poetry book. You may want to use humorous poems or poems that support a current theme in science or social studies.

Students enjoy reading books used in lessons on their own later.

Lesson 2:
Introducing the Concept of Visualizing

This Little Light of Mine
E. B. Lewis: Illustrator
Simon & Schuster, 2005

Learning objective:
Students will define visualizing and articulate the importance of mental images in strategic reading.

In this book, realistic pictures accompany the words to an old hymn. The pictures show an African-American boy helping many people in his small, rural community. From giving his mother a big hug to helping an elderly neighbor pick up spilled groceries, the boy's actions create expressions of joyful radiance on the characters' faces. Eventually, the young boy happens upon another boy, slumped over and looking forlorn outside of their small town store. The young boy invites the sad boy to come play with some of his friends and everyone ends up having fun. I love this book because it includes no words other than the lyrics of the hymn. Students will have a difficult time drawing images of the text. This challenge will reinforce the idea that descriptive text is necessary for a reader to create accurate mental images—and boost comprehension. Authors help readers to determine meaning by including descriptive language in their books. This lesson also allows time for fostering an awareness of and developing a definition of visualizing. The end result is that students are better able to apply the skill of visualizing to their independent reading.

Materials
This Little Light of Mine—wrapped in a book cover
Large piece of butcher paper posted in reading area
A sheet of 11 x 18-inch white construction paper for each team
Markers

What to Do

1. Wrap the book in a cover. Draw a large question mark on the cover and set the book on display before school starts. This mystery will pique students' curiosity. Be sure they understand not to peek inside the book. Tell them it is "top secret until further notice."

I chose *This Little Light of Mine* to introduce visualizing for several reasons. First and most important, the pictures are emotionally compelling and thought provoking. They beautifully contrast with the simple text. Second, when I read the words without showing the pictures, students realize how dependent meaning is on imagery and descriptive language.

2. Invite students to sit close to you before reading the book. Say to them, "I am going to read this book to you without showing you the pictures. Do you think you will still understand it?" Listen for comments to establish if students understand the importance of author description. If they cannot come to this point, simply continue with the lesson. They will discover this concept within the lesson.

> I tell students to think about what is happening, picturing it in their minds while I read. I also tell them I won't show them the pictures until later, but they will see if they have some pictures in their minds by just hearing the text. We talk about the "white board" in their brain where they can "draw" what the author tells them.

3. Ask students to remain silent as you read, so they don't put their ideas in someone else's head. (Allow for giggling.)

4. Read the story. It is repetitive and devoid of detail. Students may begin to chuckle, because the text consists mostly of the refrain, "This little light of mine, I'm gonna let it shine."

Trey looking over
This Little Light of Mine.

It is entertaining to watch their expressions. By the time I am halfway through the book, I usually hear, "Mrs. Z, you are tricking us!" After saying "This little light of mine, I'm gonna let it shine . . . " over and over they usually begin to giggle in happy frustration. Most find it impossible to develop pictures in their minds at all.

5. Finish reading and have students form groups of three or four. Each group will need one piece of white construction paper and markers. Ask students to collaboratively draw a picture that they imagine might be in the book and to write a paragraph as a group about why they drew that picture. Telling students other teams should not know or hear their ideas controls noise level.

6. Allow 10 to 15 minutes of work time. Circulate to listen to student conversations about the meaning of the book. You will most likely hear expressions of confusion and frustration. Expressions of doubt are important here—you want students to realize how hard this task is when an author's words provide no imagery. Lead them to this idea during the class discussion.

ADAM: Mrs. Zimny, we're confused. We don't know what to draw.
ME: Well, you listened to the story. Now draw something that is probably in
                 the book.
ADAM: But the author really didn't say anything. Just the same thing over and over.

ME: What did the author say?

BRIAN: He said there's a light and it's shining.

ME (with an impish smile): OK. So now what?

BRIAN: But that's not enough to have any real picture in my mind.

ME: And so what would you need to determine that?

7. Meet back in the reading area. Allow each team to present what it believes is the meaning of the book. Post team pictures and explanations on the large butcher paper.

This is the fun part. I hear everything from a space book about the sun's power, to lightning, to candles and fireflies and lighthouses.

8. Read the text with pictures.

As we read, we discuss each page and tell what we think is happening. This is a perfect time to bring up the word *infer* to front-load for later lessons on the strategy of making inferences. The author doesn't come out and tell us his message, but we can use clues in the pictures to determine possible meaning. When we make personal connections, we can visualize the story even better. Then, at the end, we discuss the true message of the book (kindness to others and living unselfishly) and discuss how this can be represented on our poster.

9. After the discussion, ask students if their understanding of the book has changed. You will see that many of them do see things differently.

10. Explain that when an author doesn't use descriptive words, it is hard to understand the book. The "white board" of our minds remains relatively blank. While we read, we should be making pictures in our minds that represent the text. This is what visualizing is. Don't forget to post a class-developed definition of visualizing on the chart for later reference. For example: Visualizing is what we do in our minds when we hear descriptions or see other pictures. When we visualize, it's like we see a movie on the white board of our minds. Visualizing helps us to understand a story and feel like we are there.

Reading Workshop Link: *While reading individually or with partners, have students document their use of visualizing in their Reading Journals or on Graphic Organizer 1: What I See When I Read (page 18).*

Secret Ingredient: This book would be phenomenal for introducing and assessing the strategy of making inferences or for developing an understanding of metaphor.

Name _____ **Graphic Organizer 1**

What I See When I Read

Book _____ Author _____

Picture on My "White Board"	Quote and Page Number

How did this help me understand the meaning of the author's words?

_____

_____

_____

_____

_____

Lesson 3:
Visualizing Story Events

The Midnight Ride of Paul Revere
Author: Henry Wadsworth Longfellow
Illustrator: Christopher Bing
Handprint Books, 2001

and

Paul Revere's Ride
Author: Henry Wadsworth Longfellow
Illustrator: Ted Rand
Dutton's Children's Books, 1990

Learning objective:
By comparing two books that have the same text, students will recognize that despite individual schemas, accurate and consistent visualizing of an author's words is essential to understanding plot and meaning.

The Midnight Ride of Paul Revere and *Paul Revere's Ride* always go hand in hand in my classroom. Longfellow's poem is the text for both books, but two different illustrators have compellingly and consistently interpreted the text. Once again, this lesson will make clear that, despite small schema differences, when we read text we want to accurately visualize the author's words to maintain clear understanding. Rand's and Bing's visualizations of this poem remain strikingly similar, reinforcing the idea that we must stay true to text to fully understand it.

The poem, written in 1861, nearly 100 years after Paul Revere's famous ride, is full of amazing imagery. The language of the poem is quite complex, so I tend to focus the story on Revere's horse, so it is not so overwhelming. Bing's book includes an abundance of facts about this historical event in the back of it. The Charleston Whigs specifically chose Brown Beauty for Revere because she was the fleetest animal in town. Revere didn't ride alone and—a surprise to me!—he was caught by the enemy, interrogated, disarmed, and eventually released. The British confiscated Brown Beauty, and she was never seen again.

Note: If you think the text may be too challenging—and it's appropriate for your class—there are many versions of *'Twas the Night Before Christmas* that may work just as well.

Materials

The Midnight Ride of Paul Revere

Paul Revere's Ride

2 side-by-side chairs in the reading area

Copies of Graphic Organizer 1: What I See When I Read, page 18 (optional)

What to Do

1. Gather students to the reading area and have them sit close to you.

2. Hold up both books and ask students how they are similar and different. Don't be surprised when they fail to notice that both books are by the same author. It is important to point this fact out before beginning. Make sure they understand the text is the same in both books, but that the books have different illustrators.

3. Invite one student to sit next to you on a chair. Give the student the Christopher Bing version. The student's task is to not show the pages in the Bing version until you have read the corresponding pages in the Rand version.

4. When I share the two books, I always read from Ted Rand's text and show the pictures as I go. It is amazing to see children figure out the illustrators' styles.

5. At the end of each Rand page, ask students what they think the Bing version will show. Wait for responses, and then have the student helper turn the book so students can see the picture and evaluate their predictions. You can have them complete Graphic Organizer 1 if you need something tangible to assess, but I prefer to just support the predictions with discussion since this is a modeling lesson. Writing while listening may distract kids, but could be solid practice for a few pages.

6. While reading, it is important to discuss how the illustrations are different and similar. Ask how each illustrator visualizes Longfellow's text. A great place to have this discussion is at the following part of the poem:

> *Then he climbed to the tower of the Old North Church,*
> *By wooden stairs, with stealthy tread,*
> *To the belfry chamber overhead,*
> *And startled the pigeons from their perch*
> *On the somber rafters, that round him made,*
> *Masses and moving shapes of shade—*
> *By the trembling ladder, steep and tall,*
> *To the highest window in the wall.*

ME: Students, how would you compare these two pictures?

OLIVIA: Well, they both put in the pigeons. You can see them flying around in both books.

TALIESSA: In both pictures, he's on the stairs.

JORDAN: One book shows stairs. The other is climbing on a ladder. But I guess it's because the book says both ladder and stairs. They just picked which one they wanted.

CAMERON: Both pictures show a dark attic. Maybe for the "shapes of shade" in it.

JASON: But there's a light in each picture. One has a moon in a window and the other has Paul Revere holding a lantern.

ELLEN: But it's weird, because in one picture you are looking up. The ladder goes way up to a window. The other picture makes you look down. You can see him way down the stairs holding the lamp.

TALIESSA: Yeah but it still looks steep either way. The poem says he climbed and it was steep and tall.

JASON: It still feels steep either way. I think they are both right.

7. You may want to set up a class T-chart on butcher paper and have a student record the differences and similarities of the illustrations in both texts for the whole class. This takes a lot of extra time, so I limit this to just a few examples.

Sometimes the pictures are almost the same, and sometimes they are vastly different. The punch comes at the very end when my helper shows his or her classmates Bing's final page: Paul Revere and Brown Beauty riding under a star-filled sky. Throughout the lesson I keep baiting them with, "You guys won't believe the last page of this book. It's amazing. I can't wait for you to see it." In the sky of this particular page, two flags can be seen. One is the first American flag of 13 stars. The other is the American flag of today. I always enjoy hearing the amazed "Whoa" that sweeps across the group when they see this fabulous illustration. It gives me goose bumps.

Reading journal reflection activity: Have students write to their classmates telling which book they liked the best and giving three reasons why. (These can be written on sticky notes first and then posted or recorded in their journals.)

This lesson takes a lot of time and discussion, but the in-depth conversation about how much visualizing depends on the reader is effective. I usually have to provide a lot of background information as we go, but I remain careful not to let too much explanation interfere with enjoyment of the poetry. This lesson would be perfect for a fifth-grade class, and it's a fun challenge for fourth. I never expect my students to grasp all of the text, but they always come away with something. And, hey, how can you go wrong with Longfellow?

Secret Ingredient: Sometimes I write different lines of this poem on 3- x 5-inch cards. Each student takes a card to illustrate. I ask them to find the words that help them create a mental picture in their mind. We post our pictures on a bulletin board as a reminder to keep our visualizing accurate and true to the text. Any descriptive poem would work well for this activity.

Lesson 4:
Scaffolding Visualization to Determine Setting

Thirteen Moons on Turtle's Back
Authors: Joseph Bruchac and Jonathan London
Illustrator: Thomas Locker
Philomel Books, 1992

Learning objective:
Students will accurately visualize setting by matching text to drawings.

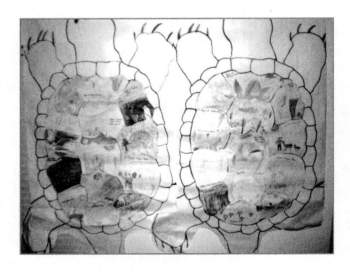

In this lesson, students create illustrations for each plate of the turtles' shells.

Thirteen Moons on Turtle's Back is a stunning poetry picture book that introduces the Native American calendar. I chose it for its multicultural flavor and descriptive language, which lends itself to visualizing of setting.

Many tribes divided the year into a series of 13 moon cycles, somewhat similar to dividing the year into 12 months. *Thirteen Moons on Turtle's Back* begins with a young boy asking Grandfather why his people have moons, instead of months. Grandfather explains that each moon represents a time period in nature. Each moon also comes with a set of tribal stories.

Each two-page spread in this lovely book includes a poem and an illustration that represents a moon. For example, the poem for the first moon is "Moon of Popping Trees," a Northern Cheyenne story. A painting of snowfields and coyotes accompanies the poem. The illustration for "Strawberry Moon," from the Seneca tribe, also shows details from the poem. In it, we see a young warrior drifting down a river in a magical canoe in early summer.

The story poems are fascinating for students of any age. My personal favorite is "Frog Moon," where Trickster asks all the animals how long winter should last, and frog says, "There should be only as many moons of snow as toes on my foot." So that is why winter is only five months long, and "when it ends, the small frogs sing their victory song in this moon with their name." (Cree tribe)

Materials

Thirteen Moons on Turtle's Back
2 large butcher-paper turtles copied from the book's dedication page
26 sheets of 11 x 18-inch white construction paper (to create puzzle pieces for each
     plate of two turtles' backs, see below)
Colored pencils or crayons
2 copies of the text of each poem

Special Lesson Preparations

* Make an overhead transparency of the turtle drawing on the dedication page.
* Project the turtle design onto a large piece of butcher paper.
* Trace the turtle onto the butcher paper and outline with black ink. (Note that the turtle shell has 13 plates; each plate represents one of the moons.)
* Use one piece of 11 x 18-inch construction paper to trace each plate, for a total of 13 plates.
* Repeat these steps so you have 2 posters, each with 13 puzzle pieces—enough for 26 students.
* Take care to number each puzzle piece with its corresponding spot on the poster.

What to Do

1. Gather students close to you on the reading carpet. Post the two large turtles on the wall behind you. At your feet, keep two copies of each poem and the puzzle pieces. Hold up the book and allow students to discuss the cover.

If this seems like a busy, heavy-duty lesson with lots of preparation, you're right. But I have found that it is well worth every step. At the end, the turtles become beautiful pieces of art that will have fellow teachers and students talking. As these posters can grace the classroom wall for the year, students never forget this lesson on visualizing.

2. Tell students this poetry book is about how some Native American tribes separated the year into moons, not the traditional months. It has a poem for each moon, from all different tribes.

3. Read the first page of the book and show students the picture of Grandfather talking with the small boy.

4. Tell them you are now going to do something unexpected. Turn to the last page of the book, titled *A Note About This Book,* and read the passages that explain how moons are equivalent to months.

5. Share the titles of the photocopied poems and tell students that they will illustrate a poem of their choice on the corresponding construction-paper puzzle piece. Tell them that you won't let them see the book's picture of their poem until after they have created their own.

6. Instruct students to take their poems and puzzle pieces back to their seats to read and illustrate.

7. Ask students to underline the words of the poem that they are drawing. This keeps students focused on illustrating the actual text.

While students work, I like to cruise the classroom to quickly assess each child's work. I check for pictures that show specific details found directly in the poem's text. The more details of the poem represented, the greater the student's power to visualize. I like to walk around and ask students whether there are clues in the poem that might reveal what season of the year it could be.

8. As students return with their work, post the puzzle pieces on the corresponding turtle butcher paper. (If there are empty places, invite some students to do two different poems.)

9. Gather together on the carpet to look at the two turtles and discuss how the turtles are similar and different. For example, puzzle piece one for First Moon may be different for both turtles, although they represent the same poem. Discuss different schemas, but also point out where both students drew what was in the text, thus making the pictures correspond.

10. Read the poems and show the text pictures. Students eagerly anticipate what their poem page will look like.

An alternative idea is to have another teacher conduct this same activity. Hang two bulletin board turtles in the hall and see what the other class develops. Kids will enjoy comparing the two turtles. I like to talk about schema at this point, and how everyone makes different pictures in their mind. Also, if I see that a student is way off track with his or her drawing, I may ask the student to label each part of the picture, reminding him or her that labels can only come from the poem. When students add things that are not in the text, I make sure to point this out.

Secret Ingredient: This is a great lesson to extend into writing workshop. Students can write their own moon poems and illustrate them. "The Moon of the Nagging Mother," created by one of my students, is still one of my favorites.

Reading Workshop Link:
As students read books on their own, ask them to pay special attention to descriptions of setting. When they come across a description of setting, ask them to illustrate the description in their reading logs or journals. I remind students to label their pictures with details from the text to ensure accuracy.

Visualizing Words and Phrases to Use in the Classroom

- White board of the brain
- Mind pictures
- Schema
- Images
- Prior experience
- Mind movies
- I see . . .

- I feel . . .
- I hear . . .
- I taste . . .
- I smell . . .
- Personification
- Metaphor
- Simile

Other Books to Teach the Visualizing Strategy

Abuela, by Arthur Dorros

Dogteam, by Gary Paulsen

Hello, Harvest Moon, by Ralph Fletcher

Twilight Comes Twice, by Ralph Fletcher

Greyling, by Jane Yolen (or anything else by her)

Aurora: A Tale of the Northern Lights, by Mindy Dwyer

Northwoods Cradle Song, by Douglas Wood

Where Would I Be in an Evergreen Tree?, by Jennifer Blomgren

Night of the Moonjellies, by Mark Shasha

Canoe Days, by Gary Paulsen

Water Dance and *Mountain Dance*, by Thomas Locker

It's Snowing! It's Snowing!, by Jack Prelutsky

The Waterfall's Gift, by Joanne Ryder

Feathers: Poems About Birds, by Eileen Spinelli

Chapter 2

Questioning/Seeking Answers

If anything comes naturally to children, it is asking questions. As teachers, we hear hundreds of questions a day to the point of exhaustion. On the very first day of school, I invite my students to ask me questions so that we can get to know one another more quickly. I think I've probably heard everything. *How tall are you? What's your real name? Do you like dogs or cats? Where did you get those weird shoes? Do you give lots of homework? When is recess?* One year I remember stopping them and saying, "Whoa! How 'bout some important questions? You know, like questions that take more than one word to answer." An intense silence fell over the class for a few moments as they processed what I said. I wondered if they knew what I was talking about when one of my boys tentatively raised his hand. *What a brave soul*, I thought. *I bet his question is a deep one.* The important question was this: "Mrs. Zimny, what color is your real hair?" Sigh. We had a long way to go.

Questioning: A Definition

In the classroom, questions are expressions of a child's curiosity and focus. Wise teachers view student questions as windows onto their thinking. Questions reveal thought process and patterns, areas of focus or distraction, and the extent of background knowledge or experience. But as Stephanie Harvey and Anne Goudvis (2000) say in their book *Strategies That Work*, "Kids don't grow up knowing that good readers ask questions. In fact, schools often appear more interested in answers than questions." I would like to add to this. Sometimes questions in school can promote passivity in learning rather than active engagement. Students should ask questions to involve them personally with text and initiate discussion. Questions can help them clarify text, develop the ability to compare and contrast, explore unfamiliar concepts, determine the importance of information, and develop an understanding of theme. When we show students that strong readers ask important questions and search text specifically for answers, we offer them another key to strategic and lifelong reading. Celebrating and encouraging student questions in the classroom turns reading passivity to active reading engagement.

Selecting Picture Books to Support Questioning Strategy Instruction

Here are some questions to ask as you choose books for strategy lessons on questioning.

- Is there a gradual release of information by the author, a technique that will encourage student questioning?
- Are topic and time period somewhat unfamiliar to students so they will be encouraged to ask questions?
- Does the book include unfamiliar cultural aspects that students will have questions about?
- Does this book offer a unique perspective that will provide opportunities for students to question and clarify points of view?
- Does the story contain inner turmoil or outer conflict so students may have questions about possible outcomes?
- Are the pictures and cover compelling enough to readers to foster questioning?
- Will students relate to the book's emotional content and be able to ask questions based on their own background experiences?
- Is an element of mystery or fantasy present to stimulate thinking and questioning?

Lesson 5:
Modeling Questioning to Determine Importance

The Scarlet Stockings Spy
Author: Trinka Hakes Noble
Illustrator: Robert Papp
Sleeping Bear Press, 2004

Learning objective:
Students will use questioning strategies to determine importance.

The themes of family, patriotism, and hope weave through *The Scarlet Stockings Spy*, a beautifully illustrated book. The heroine, Maddy Rose, is a young girl in the fall of 1777. The tension of the Revolutionary War grips her hometown of colonial Philadelphia. Outside her bedroom window, she can see the harbor beginning to fill with British men-o-war, while her 15-year-old brother encamps outside of town with Washington's army. At night, brother Jonathan sneaks to his sister's house to look at her clothesline, which has become a code system between the siblings. By the laundry hung upon it, Jonathan can tell which ships are present, as well as their positions in the harbor. Maddy Rose hangs white petticoats to signify Patriot vessels. Red stockings mean British ships are near. A red stocking with a cobblestone in the toe means a British ship is sitting low in the water, heavy with artillery.

The tension and pathos of the story rises when Jonathan does not appear one night. Maddy waits night after night, refusing to believe her young brother is dead. Eventually, Seth, the new American spy who has replaced her brother, appears. He informs Maddy that her brother fell in battle. He gives her a package. It is Jonathan's blue coat, complete with a bullet hole in the chest.

The story ends with the Patriots triumphantly driving the British from Philadelphia and early American flags flying along the waterfront. From Maddy's house, a flag made of petticoats, red stockings, and a blue uniform waves in the wind. There is a musket ball hole in the piece, right under one of the stars.

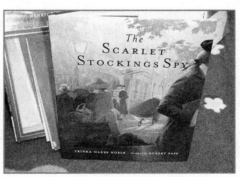

Our lesson book on display.

Materials
The Scarlet Stockings Spy
Large piece of butcher paper with Graphic Organizer 2 copied onto it
Copies of Graphic Organizer 2: Questions and Answers About the Cover Picture, page 32 (optional)

What to Do

1. Before the lesson, prepare a class graphic organizer chart for questioning book covers (see page 32) and post nearby. I use this first to record student questions and later the answers we find as we read. You can also choose to have students fill out the graphic organizers as you read.

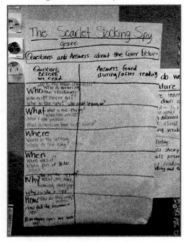

Our Five W's and How chart for *The Scarlet Stockings Spy*.

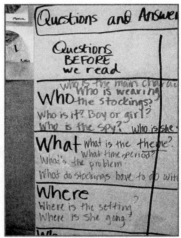

2. Inform students that good readers begin asking questions as soon as they pick up a book—maybe even before they open it. By asking questions about a book's cover, we can begin to focus on the important elements of plot.

Starting with just a book's cover is not as overwhelming as taking on the whole book. It gives direct focus and purpose to the lesson, while keeping the task simple.

3. Share the cover of *The Scarlet Stockings Spy* with students.

The cover of this book shows an eighteenth-century street scene with a young girl hurrying through the crowd. She's wearing an intriguing pair of scarlet stockings that get students asking questions right away. The costumes of other characters and the street are also unfamiliar, fostering questions about when and where the story takes place.

4. Ask them to quietly think about the "Five W's and How." I remain quiet at this time and simply record the questions. I try to remember that the point of questioning is to inspire discussion and determine importance.

I point to the posted graphic organizer and explain that the Five W's are *who, what, where, when,* and *why.* Support students by telling them to think of questions that may start with one of these words. Remind them that these questions help us to focus on the important parts of a book's plot. I record their questions on the left side of the chart. You will hear students make side comments as the list develops.

AMBER: Why is there a spy?

JASON: Who is the spy and why is he there?

JESSICA: How come there's a spy? Is he bad?

CAMERON: Why are there scarlet stockings? Will the spy wear them?

JESSICA: Maybe the spy will steal them. Maybe they're worth a lot of money.

JASON: Well, why are they scarlet? Does that mean red? I see the red socks
           on the cover.

JESSICA: They're scarlet because they're worth a lot of money. I bet they're magic.

AMBER: Why does the spy have to be a boy?

5. Direct student questions to the picture on the cover. Add questions about the cover to the chart.

Sample Questions

> **Where does this take place? In a town?**
> **When does it take place? A long time ago?**
> **Why do the men dress like the women?**
> **Why is the person with the stockings running away?**
> **Who is the main character? The spy?**
> **Where is he going?**
> **Who is he? Is it a boy or a girl?**
> **What is he doing? Did he steal something? Is he afraid?**
> **What are all those other people doing?**

By the way, illustrator Robert Papp gets all the credit for this amazingly detailed book. His acrylic paintings are mesmerizing. One of my students said, "Those people in the pictures look almost real." I think much of the impact of the story comes from the dramatic artwork.

6. Allow students to keep questioning as you read, but don't take up time by adding these questions to the chart. Listen to be sure students can ask authentic questions using the Five W's and How. Questions should pertain to the important plot elements of the story.

While reading, students will point out answers to the questions on the chart. Simply record answers on the chart and continue reading. You know you are empowering readers when you hear excited chatter as answers are discovered. Students are learning that reading is active and a joyful discovery. You are also pre-assessing your students' abilities to formulate questions and actively seek answers. A distinction between strong and challenged readers may appear. I gently encourage my challenged readers by calling on them and allowing lots of think time. Long hesitations and withdrawal tells me this strategy needs to be reinforced during one-on-one conference time.

Secret Ingredient: There are many similes in this text, so it lends itself to a writing lesson on figurative language.

Name ————————————————————— **Graphic Organizer 2**

Questions and Answers About the Cover Picture

Book ———————————————— Author ————————————————

Questions Before We Read	Answers Found During/After Reading
Who?	
What?	
Where?	
When?	
Why?	
How?	

Lesson 6:
Scaffolding Student Questioning of Text

Train to Somewhere
Author: Eve Bunting
Illustrator: Ronald Himler
Clarion Books, 1996

Learning objective:
Students will use the questioning strategy for clarification during reading.

When I first discovered *Train to Somewhere*, I hesitated to share it with my fourth graders. I thought it might seem too slow for them because much of the conflict is internal and the theme is more mature. Then I realized that the book would make an excellent choice for teaching the questioning strategy because of the gradual release of information by the author. Gradual release of information occurs when an author withholds crucial details from the reader in order to develop a temporary state of confusion, suspicion, or mystery. Written by reputable and talented author Eve Bunting, the book is alive with emotion as it explores universal issues such as mother-daughter relationships, loneliness, and fear. It turned out my students loved this book, becoming completely fascinated with the concept of orphan trains. I had another one of those lumps in my throat the whole time reading it. It is now one of my top picture books for fourth graders.

Giving students time to talk about stories with peers increases their comprehension and interest.

The book is about a homeless girl named Marianne and her journey west on an orphan train to find a real home. She travels with 14 other children and kind Mrs. Randolph, their caseworker. As Marianne travels through each small town, she hopes to see her mother waiting for her. She remembers her mother well and recalls her mother's promise to return for her. Eventually, she comes to terms with the fact that her mother is gone, possibly dead, and she seeks to simply be adopted. We watch her deal with rejection at every train stop. In the end she is the only child remaining. The town is called Somewhere, and a kind elderly couple take to her immediately. The book ends with the signing of "agreement papers." The readers are left to predict how the rest of Marianne's life will unfold.

Materials
Train to Somewhere
Large piece of butcher paper titled "Our Questions"

What to Do

1. Gather students and introduce *Train to Somewhere*.

2. As you read the book, record questions on a chart as follows:

We Are Learning About:

How Good Readers Ask Questions When They Read

What does "placing out" mean? (Rylee)

I wonder who she wants to be waiting for her? (Tamika)

What is the feather all about? (Trey)

Why does she keep the feather in her pocket? (Ben)

Is the feather special? (Keenan)

Where are they going? (Monica)

Why does she say "Mama?" I thought they were orphans! (Robbie)

I'm wondering—did her mom leave her? (Keenan)

Why do they want the kids? (Cruz)

Will they treat them like slaves? (Robbie)

How did the feather get in her mother's hair? (Monica)

I make sure to record students' names next to their questions. This helps each student feel like he or she is part of the lesson. It also encourages students to remember their question and look specifically for its answer while we share the book. I take care not to interrupt the story too much. Sometimes I hold off questions until we reach the bottom of each page or I may read up to page 8 and solicit questions at that point.

3. Once we finish reading the text, we revisit our question chart to see if any were answered. We discover that some questions definitely were, so we record the answers on the chart, or simply mark an "A" for "answered" next to the question.

I believe *Train to Somewhere* is so powerful in the classroom because it strongly lends itself to heavy-duty questioning in the beginning pages. I try to remember that the goal of a strategy lesson is to increase comprehension, not interrupt it. Our lessons should always reflect authentic use of comprehension strategies. There are moments when readers should simply enjoy a book and allow the story to unfold. Fade out questions as you reach the middle of *Train to Somewhere* and encourage students to just listen and enjoy. This models pacing. Pacing is knowing when to apply strategies and when to hold off to experience the impact of the story and become immersed in the author's flow of writing.

In my experience when teaching this book, the emotion tends to pile up as each page turns. When this happens, you know you are sharing high-quality literature with your students. Questioning tends to ease as readers become engrossed. You will see questions die off as students become deeply immersed in the story—glued to each word in utter silence. We discuss how there is a time to question and a time just to absorb the story.

Secret Ingredient: There exist myriad teaching possibilities when using *Train to Somewhere* in the classroom. I use it primarily for teaching questioning, but it is an excellent toe dip into the strategy of making inferences, a strategy I teach immediately after questioning. My students and I read this book while conducting a whole-class literature circle on *Sarah, Plain and Tall* by Patricia MacLachlan. We create a Venn diagram and compare the two stories or the two main characters, Sarah with Marianne. Think about comparing *Train to Somewhere* with *Dandelions*, another Bunting title. Both books explore the concept of family and the human struggle to make one's way in life.

Lesson 7:
Scaffolding Questioning to Determine Important Elements of a Narrative Story

The Widow's Broom
Author and Illustrator: Chris Van Allsburg
Houghton Mifflin, 1992

Learning objective:

Students will use the questioning strategy to discover the important elements of a narrative story.

In this lesson, we create a chart that explores the elements of a story.

While flying through the night sky, a witch's broom runs out of magic and falls to the earth in the surreal book *The Widow's Broom*. The expired broom and its unlucky passenger crash into a lonely widow's garden. Minna Shaw takes pity upon the injured witch and nurses her back to health. When the mysterious houseguest recovers at last, she disappears upon the broom of another witch without so much as a good-bye. The old broom is left behind, but Widow Shaw soon discovers it has a bit of magic left in it. It sweeps her home, chops wood, and entertains her in the evening with some piano playing. They live in relative peace and quiet until a nearby farmer by the name of Spivey becomes fearful of the broom's magic and rallies the neighborhood for a good old-fashioned broom burning. The widow wisely gives him a regular household broom as a substitute, and she and the real magic broom devise a plan to scare Spivey and his children away for good. The plan works, and the story ends happily. I always love reading this wonderful book and listening to my students squeal with laughter when the magic broom flings the Spiveys' dog, played by Van Allsburg's famous bull terrier, Fritz, high into the air.

Chris Van Allsburg books never fail me in reading strategy lessons. His stories move between the worlds of reality and fantasy, and they are always intriguing. Although suitable at any time of year, we read *The Widow's Broom* just before Halloween. Like many of Van Allsburg's books, it inevitably becomes a favorite with students year after year.

Materials

1 or more copies of *The Widow's Broom*
Large piece of butcher paper posted near
    the reading area
Markers
White sheets of 11 x 18-inch drawing paper
    for each team

You will also need two sets of five 3- x 5-inch cards, each marked with one of the following questions:

Who are the characters?
Where and when does the story take place?
What is the problem or conflict in the story?
How is the problem or conflict resolved?
Why did the author write this?

An optional sixth card could read: *What elements of fantasy are included in this story?*

Common Elements of Fantasy

- The plot involves magical objects, people, or animals.
- The magic can be either good or bad.
- The number three may occur throughout the story.
- The setting may be in the distant past, with elements of historical fiction.
- The setting may take place in unusual and strange worlds.
- Good battles evil and usually triumphs.
- Anthropomorphism (where animals act like people) may be present.
- Most endings are happy and teach a life lesson to the reader.

- Adapted from www.readwritethink.org

What to Do

1. Introduce *The Widow's Broom*, asking students to volunteer titles of any other Chris Van Allsburg books they know, such as *Jumanji*, *Zathura*, or *The Garden of Abdul Gasazi*. Allow a few moments to discuss students' experiences with these other books.

2. Have students form teams of three or four. Tell them that while you read the story, each team will be listening for answers to an important question about narrative elements, such as character, setting, problem presented, problem solution, and theme. You may want to add the question about the elements of fantasy if you need another group, or if you want to go further in the text.

Questioning Elements in a Story

Book ———————————————————— Author ————————————————————

Who are the characters?	**What is the setting?**
What are the problems or conflicts?	**How is the conflict or problem solved?**

Why do you think the author wrote this book?

—Adapted from Debbie Miller's *Reading With Meaning* (2002).

Using Picture Books to Teach Comprehension Strategies

3. When I introduce these narrative elements to the class, I post each of the question cards from one set in a separate section of the butcher paper. I believe this serves as a visual reminder to students about the parts of a story. By looking at the butcher paper divided into sections, students realize that all the elements make up a whole story.

4. Pass out one card from the other set you made to each group. Tell the groups that while you read the story, they should be thinking about how to answer their question for the class.

5. Read the story and enjoy the impact it has on students. I like this book because it is one of Allsburg's lesser-known titles. Most students will find this book a novelty. The bizarre incident at the beginning hooks students immediately, but the universal childhood experience of bullying helps them relate to the storyline despite the strangeness.

6. After listening to the story, send groups back to tables to work on their questions. Tell students they will need to draw a picture to represent their answer and also write a paragraph that explains it. I remind students that they must include details from the text to support what they draw and write. I emphasize ideas must always be supported. This is an ongoing challenge with all students. They have to remember to not only tell *what* they know, but *why* they know it.

7. Each team attaches its paragraph to the poster, and then presents to the rest of the class. As teams come up to share what they wrote and drew, we discuss the story even more deeply.

Reading Workshop Link:
Students can use Graphic Organizer 3: Questioning Elements in a Story (page 38)
with their independent reading books for additional practice.

Secret Ingredient: *The Widow's Broom* is an especially good book to use for teaching about the literary element of mood.

Lesson 8:
Scaffolding Questions to Determine Character Traits

The Talking Eggs
Author: Robert San Souci
Illustrator: Jerry Pinkney
Dial Books, 1989

Learning objective:

Using the reading strategy of questioning, students will compare and contrast two important characters in a narrative.

Winner of the Coretta Scott King Award and the Caldecott Honor, *The Talking Eggs* will get your kids squealing with delight over every bizarre page. A Creole folk tale set in the American South, *The Talking Eggs* is a Cinderella story with twists and turns and lots of cultural impact. It works well for scaffolding the questioning strategy because of the fascinating, surreal events that occur and the very different personalities of the two sisters. Pinkney's illustrations and San Souci's word choice combine to create a wonderful expression of Creole culture. Because Creole culture is unfamiliar to many students, the book also provides ample opportunities for practicing the questioning strategy.

On a farm that "look(s) like the tail end of bad luck," young Blanche lives with her cruel mother and sister Rose in debilitating poverty. Because of their poor treatment of her, Blanche's life becomes increasingly unbearable. One day, after being sent to the well for water, Blanche meets a mysterious old woman and kindly offers her a drink. Beaten when she returns home for taking so long, Blanche decides to run away. While traveling through the forest, she meets the elderly woman again and allows herself to be taken to the woman's cabin in the woods. There she sees the most amazing sights, such as dancing rabbits, cows with twisty horns, and the old woman removing her head to brush her long gray hair. Eventually, the woman, or "aunty," as Blanche affectionately now refers to her, allows Blanche to take some eggs from the henhouse. Blanche is careful to take only the plain eggs as promised and not the beautifully decorated ones. The aunty tells Blanche to drop the eggs over her shoulders as she walks home. The eggs break and reveal incredible treasures.

When Blanche returns home, Rose and Mama see the newfound treasures and burn with jealousy. After Blanche falls asleep, Rose tracks down the aunty and insists on taking eggs. But greed gets the best of her and she grabs the fancy eggs despite being warned to take only the plain ones. Dropping the eggs over her shoulders on the way home, beasts of every kind emerge to teach her a lesson.

Materials

The Talking Eggs

A piece of butcher paper labeled "Questions About Characters"

Markers

What to Do

1. Call students to the reading area and show them the cover of *The Talking Eggs*. Point out the butcher paper and its title "Questions About Characters" behind you. At this point I like to say, "Today we are going to use our questioning skills to find out about characters. Knowing about characters is an important part of understanding a story. Questioning why people do and say things helps us understand them better. Remember that sometimes authors use characters to give us a hint about the theme of a story."

2. Share the cover of the book to help students formulate some questions and predict what the topic of the book may be.

3. Read page one where the two sisters are introduced, and stop. On the butcher paper, draw a T-chart. Label the left side "Blanche" and the right side "Rose."

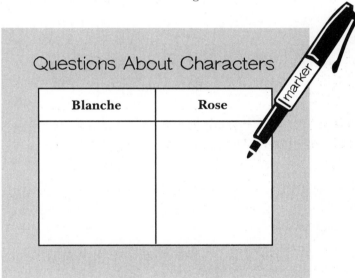

4. After the first page, ask students to volunteer questions about Blanche, based on what she says and does. Record the questions under her name.

5. Ask students to ask questions about Rose, also thinking about what she says and does. Record them under her name.

Questions About Characters

Blanche	Rose
Why does she have to do all the work?	Why is she so mean?
Is she mad about it?	Is she her mom's favorite?
Why does she do what they say?	What does it mean that she "didn't know beans from birds' eggs"?
Aren't some of her chores dangerous?	Why does she just talk about fancy balls and getting rich all day?
Does she want to run away?	Why doesn't she like her sister?
Doesn't her mom love her?	Does she ever help?
What does it mean when you are "sharp as forty crickets"?	

6. Continue reading the book. Stop periodically and list more questions about the two characters. About midway, students become more engrossed in the story and questions will taper off. This is to be expected. They may want to point out answers or share opinions about the two characters. Discussion while reading is essential to modeling comprehension, but I tend to phase it out once we pass the middle of a book. Simple enjoyment of the book is foremost.

Note: I love to make the eggs sing "Take me!" or "Don't take me!" in squeaky little voices. This always gets students laughing, and I get to brush up on my dramatic skills. Reading should be a celebration. Go for great acting!

7. After reading, I have students write a paragraph comparing the two sisters. Some teachers may be more comfortable with a Venn diagram at first, but I find that the discussion and questions well prepare students for this task. You may want to call them back to the reading carpet to share paragraphs and have them attach the paragraphs to the poster for further reference. The paragraphs may be used as an assessment as well.

Reading Workshop Link:

As students read on their own, ask them to record questions about characters in their Reading Journals, focusing on what the characters do and say and how they are described. Remind students to go back to see if they find the answers to their questions as they continue reading.

Sample Reflection Ideas on Questioning

✱ Which questions helped you understand the story?

✱ How did these questions help you?

✱ Why do you think the author wrote this book? In other words, what is the secret message, or theme, for kids? Explain your answer.

✱ How will you use questioning strategies in the future?

✱ What is the most important thing you learned about questioning?

✱ What still confuses you?

Secret Ingredient: You can use *The Talking Eggs* when discussing voice in writing workshop.

Lesson 9:
Asking Literal and Inferential Questions

The Other Side
Author: Jacqueline Woodson
Illustrator: E. B. Lewis
Putnam, 2001

Learning Objective:
Students will practice asking literal and inferential questions to increase comprehension of text.

**Our lesson book
on display.**

The Other Side is an absolute must in every classroom. I found it a few years ago while cruising the bookstore and immediately fell in love with the pictures, powerful message, and its kid-friendly presentation of a serious issue. The symbolism of the fence separating the girls fosters inferential thinking.

Clover, a young African-American girl, narrates the story. She plays in her yard with friends and apparently leads the idyllic, innocent life of many American children. And yet, the foreboding words of her mother haunt the scene: "And Mama said, 'Don't climb over that fence when you play.' She said it wasn't safe." Your students will wonder what the "unsafe" thing could be.

The last page of the book is fabulous. It reads:

"Someday somebody's going to come along
And knock this old fence down," Annie said.
And I nodded, "Yeah," I said. "Someday."

**Peer support develops a positive,
safe environment for risk-taking.**

Materials
The Other Side
Large piece of butcher paper
Markers

What to Do

1. Gather students close to you and introduce *The Other Side* by studying the cover together.

2. Point out the butcher paper hanging nearby. Explain that today you will be talking about different kinds of questions.

Teamwork is essential in a literacy-rich classroom.

3. Ask students to ask questions about the cover. List these on the butcher paper. Continue reading the book and recording questions.

The Other Side Questions

> Why is there a fence between them?
> Are they fighting?
> Is it in the country?
> What are their names?
> Why is it not safe?
> Why is the girl standing there?
> Will the other girls be mean to her?

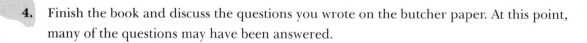

4. Finish the book and discuss the questions you wrote on the butcher paper. At this point, many of the questions may have been answered.

5. Ask students which questions the author answered in the story. Tell students these are *literal questions* because these can be answered by looking right in the text. Go through the class list and allow students to mark an L next to literal questions.

6. Point out the questions that were not marked. Tell students that the author did not give us answers, but she may have given us some clues. Taking the clues from the story and using what we already know can help us discover answers to these questions. This is called *inferring*, and questions that ask us to think like that are called *inferential questions*. Have students mark the inferential questions on the chart with an I. Discuss answers. Inferential questions are important because they lead us into the meaning of the story.

Secret Ingredient: Use the book for teaching the writing trait of voice. Also, to check for individual understanding, bring out the chart of questions students made with *The Scarlet Stockings Spy*. Ask them to take a few minutes to label these as literal or inferential questions.

Lesson 10:
Assessment of Literal and Inferential Questioning

Virgie Goes to School With Us Boys
Author: Elizabeth Fitzgerald Howard
Illustrator: E. B. Lewis
Simon & Schuster, 2000

Learning objective:
Students will practice asking literal and inferential questions while reading.

Another Coretta Scott King Award recipient, *Virgie Goes to School With Us Boys* is perfect for practicing the questioning strategy. It is also a true story, which never fails to leave students incredulous. The idea of not having access to school because of one's skin color fascinates them. In the story, a young girl named Virgie begs her previously enslaved parents allow her to go to school with her five brothers. The brothers continually remind her that she is "scarcely as big as a field mouse" and that she would probably cry for her mama. Although the walk to school is seven miles long, her father agrees to let her go, saying, "All free people need learning—old folks, young folks . . . and small girls, too." So her mother packs six buckets of food (they have to make it last the whole week) and sends the children off. Virgie must face the terrifying woods on the way there, where her brother, who teases that Raw Head and Old Bloody Bones are lying in wait for her. She makes it through alive, of course, and meets the Quaker family that is running the school for the children of freed slaves. For the first time in her life, Virgie touches a book.

Materials
1 or more copies of *Virgie Goes to School With Us Boys*
1 or more copies of *The Other Side*
Notebook paper for each student
Clipboards

What to Do

1. Gather students closely to you. Show them the chart paper created in the last lesson of *The Other Side*.

2. Review the definitions of literal and inferential questions and discuss their importance when comprehending text.

3. Tell students that today they will listen quietly to another book illustrated by E. B. Lewis. They won't be able to make comments, but they will be able to write.

4. Pass out clipboards and a sheet of paper to each student. While you read the book, have students record questions they have about the story.

5. Stop reading at the point when Virgie and her brothers reach the forest. Ask students to set their clipboards aside until the book is finished.

6. Finish reading the book. Send students back to their seats, asking them to label their questions as literal or inferential.

7. For reflection, at the bottom of their papers, have students write how their questions helped them understand the story better. For an extension, ask them to answer their questions if they can.

8. Collect papers and check for understanding. The guide below will help you score their work. A delightful part of this book is the author's note at the end. The text is a true story about life

---

Assessing Student Questioning: A Scoring Guide

4: Poses probing, elaborating, and divergent questions to challenge the validity of print, author stance/point of view, clarify nuances of meaning, and determine the controlling idea or theme. Eloquently explains how questioning aids comprehension.

3: Poses questions to challenge the validity of print, author stance/point of view, clarify nuances of meaning, and determine the controlling idea or theme. Adequately explains how questioning aids comprehension.

2: Poses literal questions to clarify meaning, but seldom frames a question to explore the controlling idea/theme or author's stance/point of view. Incompletely explains how questioning aids comprehension.

1: Poses irrelevant questions. Unable to coherently explain how questioning aids comprehension.

0: Poses no questions. Offers no explanation of how questioning aids comprehension.

— Adapted by Valerie Bush of Central Kitsap School District from *Mosaic of Thought* (1997) by Ellin Oliver Keene and Susan Zimmermann.

in Tennessee. As it turns out, brother C. C. is author Howard's grandfather. All of the boys grow up and later attend college. Despite their hardships, two grow up to become lawyers, one a doctor, and one a pharmacist. What happens to Virgie? She grows up to marry the president of Jarvis Christian College in Texas, but unfortunately dies at the early age of 30.

Secret Ingredient: *Virgie Goes to School With Us Boys* is an excellent book to compare and contrast with *The Other Side*. Both texts carry the theme of struggling to overcome severe limitations imposed by society. Because E. B. Lewis illustrates both books, discuss the differences and similarities of the artwork. This book also works well for teaching the trait of voice in writing workshop.

Other Books to Teach the Questioning Strategy

Coming on Home Soon, by Jacqueline Woodson

The Star Spangled Banner, by Amy Winstead

Imagine a Night, by Rob Gonsalves and Sarah L. Thomson

The Light of Christmas, by Richard Paul Evans

The Blizzard, by Betty Ren Wright

Dandelions, by Eve Bunting

A Is for Africa, by Ifeoma Onyefulu

Mother to Tigers, by George Ella Lyon

Ashanti to Zulu: African Traditions, by Margaret Musgrove

Winter's Gift, by Jane Monroe Donovan

When Jessie Came Across the Sea, by Amy Hest

The Sea Chest, by Toni Buzzeo

Chapter 3

Making Inferences

It was snowing. To many teachers, falling snow is a typical event during the winter months, but in western Washington it's cause for mass hysteria. The infrequent occurrence of snow creates a flurry of activity and much exhilaration within classrooms. From kindergarten to 12th grade, students monitor each flake that passes the classroom window and hope that school will be canceled. This distraction typically renders all attempts to teach exercises in futility, but on this particular day I still had a lot to get done before the buses got their tires chained.

I called students over to read Eve Bunting's book *The Memory String* (2002). As I started the book, pink-cheeked students were still fidgeting after their last venture onto the whitening playground. Surprisingly, after the first pages, my students settled down and became absolutely silent, as if a spell had come over them. As I continued to read, the silence held fast. Finally, as I turned another page, Rylee whispered to herself, "I know about this." It suddenly occurred to me that my students had made personal connections to Bunting's emotional tale about accepting a new stepmom. My students had used their own personal experiences and Bunting's descriptive clues about characters' body language, words, and actions to make inferences. Students knew the conflict in *The Memory String* was complicated and heart wrenching without Bunting coming out and saying it.

Making Inferences: A Definition

According to Ellin Oliver Keene and Susan Zimmermann (2007), early proponents of strategy instruction, to *infer* means to go beyond the literal text by using one's own personal experiences to create a new, deeper understanding. They state, "Inferring is a tool we use to go beyond text, to leverage prior knowledge and create connections among various details and concepts we have learned, to draw conclusions based on the text and our full array of life experience and knowledge. Without inferring, we may be condemned to remember only phone numbers, padlock combinations, and plant names" (p. 152). Inferring is a vital strategy for readers because it enables us to draw conclusions, analyze characters and plot, and determine theme. It moves students past literal meanings and into the deeper realms of an author's purpose.

Selecting Picture Books to Support Inferring Instruction

Here are some questions to ask as you choose picture books for teaching the strategy of making inferences.

- Is there a gradual release of information by the author, providing opportunities for students to infer—and later validate their inferences?
- Will the book's unfamiliar topic or time period encourage students to infer in order to determine meaning?
- Does the book have a compelling cover that will encourage students to infer about its content or plot?
- Is the book part of a series by the same author, giving students a chance to compare and contrast several titles?
- Does the story contain inner turmoil or outer conflict that students can infer based on characters' speech, actions, or body language?
- Does the book contain a life message that must be inferred?
- Is an element of mystery or fantasy present to stimulate making inferences?
- Does the author use details to express an important point rather than stating it plainly?

Lesson 11:
Defining and Modeling Making Inferences

The Memory String
Author: Eve Bunting
Illustrator: Ted Rand
Clarion Books, 2000

Learning objective:
Students will practice and define the strategy of making inferences and tell
how it can help readers understand text.

A few years ago, *The Memory String* by Eve Bunting was my hot find. It was another book I wasn't too sure about, since the pictures seemed a little young for fourth graders. Initially purchasing it for the narrative plot elements of conflict and resolution, I soon realized Bunting cleverly refuses to come directly out to explain her characters or their problems. She depends on description of body language, plot action, and character speech to develop conflict, character, and theme. Through her clues and our personal experiences, we can determine meaning in this complex story.

The story opens with young Laura sitting under a tree with her cat, Whiskers. Dad and stepmom Jane are busy painting the porch. Laura refuses to join them and continues to sit on the grass counting the buttons she keeps on a string. She explains to her cat, loudly so that the resented Jane can hear, what each button represents. One button is from her mother's nightgown, taken before she died. Another is from her father's uniform when he was in the Gulf War. Each button represents something (or someone) important in Laura's life.

The tension can be inferred from the pictures as well as the conversation between Jane and Laura. Laura is shown purposely sitting away from Jane. They speak in short sentences while Laura glares at Jane from beneath a tree. The awkward situation becomes even more difficult when Whiskers breaks the string and the buttons fly in every direction. Jane and Father help to find the buttons, but one remains lost. It is the button from Father's uniform.

That night, Laura overhears her father and Jane talking. Her father wants to solve the missing button problem by simply taking another button off of his uniform. Jane, however, insists that would be dishonest. "No substitutes," she reminds him, in words that seem to apply to mothers as well.

In any case, Jane searches the yard with a flashlight and finds the button. She leaves it on the porch for Laura to find on her own. Of course, Laura knows this. In the morning, she asks Jane to help her fix the string. The beginning of hope for their relationship remains unspoken, but it is evident in the characters' words and actions.

Materials

1 or more copies of *The Memory String*

A large piece of butcher paper posted in reading area

Markers

Copies of Graphic Organizer 4: Inferring Character and Conflict, page 53

What to Do

1. Call students over to the reading area and introduce *The Memory String*.

2. Point out the butcher paper posted nearby. Say, "We will use this chart to track clues from the story. The author doesn't come right out and tell us what the characters are like or what the problem is. We have to use our own experiences and clues in the story to find out the meaning."

3. On the chart write: Inferring Character and Conflict. Below the chart title, create three columns:

   1. Character Name
   2. What the Character Does/Says
   3. Our Inference

4. Read the first page and stop. Begin to fill out the chart with students. Encourage students to use their own experience to decide what may be happening. Ask, "What are the characters Laura and Jane doing and saying here?" Record their names in the first column.

MAGGIE: They're painting, but not Laura. She's sitting by herself under the tree.

JARED: The stepmom Jane asks Laura if she wants lemonade, but Laura shakes her head no.

MAX: Yeah, and then the girl pulls out a string of buttons, but she makes sure her stepmom sees her do it. The stepmom gets stiff shoulders.

ME: OK. Let's look in the third column. Here it says "Our Inference." In other words, what do we think may be happening here?

MAGGIE: I think Laura is pouting or something when she won't take the lemonade.

MAX: Yeah, and I think the stepmom is a little mad at her.

JARED: But the stepmom is smiling in the picture.

Inferring Character and Conflict

Book _____ Author _____

Character Name	What the Character Does/Says	My Inference

MAX: But it says her shoulders were stiff. I think she was mad or something.

MAGGIE: She's probably just smiling to make Laura come over to her.

ME: OK. Tell me how you know this. I mean, how do you know that Laura is pouting?

MAGGIE: Well, I know Laura's pouting. She doesn't even answer her stepmom. She just sits away from them. And look at her face in the picture.

JARED: She looks sad, but why is the stepmom smiling?

MAX: I know she's mad. It says her shoulders are stiff. I think it's because it says Laura pulled out the button string a lot when Jane looks over. I think this makes Jane mad. She probably only smiles when she offers the lemonade. She's trying to be nice about it.

5. Continue reading, filling out the chart when students have something to offer.

Name _____ **Graphic Organizer 4**

Inferring Character and Conflict

Book _____ Author _____

Character Name	What the Character Does/Says	My Inference
Laura	*Laura sits by herself and refuses lemonade. The stepmom gets stiff shoulders when Laura pulls out a string of buttons. Laura has a pouty face in the picture. Everybody gets quiet when Laura takes out the string of buttons. Even the cat's tail is twitching!*	*Laura's pouting, but the stepmom wants to be nice. Laura is being mean when she shows the string of buttons. It's probably from her real mom and that makes Jane mad. Everybody seems mad. Laura probably doesn't like her stepmom*

6. At the end, talk about the author's purpose for writing the book. What is she trying to tell kids? What's the life lesson we are supposed to get from her story? Explain this as a book's theme. When students suggest the author's purpose for the book, make sure they can also provide support from the text.

7. As a class, develop a definition for the strategy of making inferences and post it near the butcher paper as a reminder.

> **Reading Workshop Link:** *While reading individually or with partners, students can use Graphic Organizer 4 on page 53 to practice this strategy. In their journals, ask them to draw two boxes. In one box, they are to record what they understand about making inferences. In the other box, they write what they are still confused about.*

Secret Ingredient: Use the book during writing workshop to model development of character or conflict/solution/outcome in narratives.

Lesson 12:
Modeling the Strategy of Making Inferences to Determine Character

The Royal Bee
Authors: Frances Park and Ginger Park
Illustrator: Christopher Zhong-Yuan Zhang
Boyds Mills Press, 2000

Learning objective:
Students will practice inferring to define a character in a story.

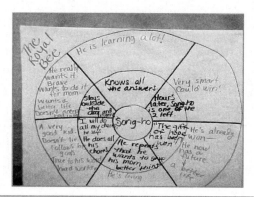

Our class chart for
The Royal Bee.

Written by two sisters about the life of their Korean grandfather named Song-ho, *The Royal Bee* is a great book for teaching the strategy of inferring to define a character. This author team carefully describes what their grandfather did and said to portray his personality traits of ambition, determination, and love. This is a high-interest story, and students will be deeply affected by the idea that poverty prevents many children from going to school.

Young Song-ho, a poor, or "sangmin," boy, works all day in the fields. He hears school bells and dreams of going to school, where he can learn to read and write poetry, but only rich "yangban" children are allowed at school. Song-ho seems doomed to a life of poverty and hard work. Then he bravely decides to sit outside the school door to listen to the teacher's lessons. Master Min, the teacher, notices him and tells him to go away. Song-ho remains outside the door to listen and Master Min, despite what he said, is careful to recite the lessons loudly for all to hear. Song-ho remains outside the door through many months, even in the winter. Finally, Master Min takes a risk and allows Song-ho to enter the classroom.

Song-ho studies along with the others and eventually reaches the top of his class. To reward him, the students make Song-ho a beautiful ceremonial costume to wear to the country's largest academic contest, the Royal Bee. There, Song-ho ties with another student. To break the tie, they must tell why they want to win and Song-ho wisely states that he wants to win for his mother, so that they may have a better life. He is able to return home to his mother with the grand prize, gold coins and a cow. The sound of school bells ringing closes the story.

Materials
1 or more copies of *The Royal Bee*
A large piece of butcher paper posted in the reading area
Markers in three different colors
Copies of Graphic Organizer 5: Targeting Character Inferences, page 57

What to Do

1.   Call students over to the reading area and show them *The Royal Bee*.

2.   Point out the definition of the strategy of making inferences that you have previously posted in the classroom.

3.   Say, "We have been learning about how strong readers make inferences when they read. This means that they think about their own experiences and make connections to the story to expand the meaning. Sometimes the author doesn't come right out and tell us what's going on. Sometimes they only give us clues."

Name _____   **Graphic Organizer 5**

Targeting Character Inferences

Book _____ Author _____

Start in the middle and work out!

My inferences about the
character based on his or her words and actions

What the character
says or does

Character

4. Draw a large, three-ring target on the butcher paper. (See Graphic Organizer 5: Targeting Character Inferences.) The idea is to start in the center and work out. In the center write the name "Song-ho." Say, "This is a story about a Korean boy who is very poor. The authors don't really come out tell us what he's like, but they use what he says and does to give us clues. Let's see if we can use our connections and the author clues to create some inferences about this boy's character."

5. Read the first page to students and look back at the chart, asking, "What has the author told us so far about Song-ho?"

   Students should mention the following:
   He dressed in rags.
   He was a sangmin boy, not a yangban.
   He dreams about being able to read and write poetry.

6. Record their comments in the second ring out from the bull's-eye. For example, write, "He was a sangmin boy dressed in rags." After recording this, move to the next outer ring from that sentence and say, "OK. What inference can we make about Song-ho when reading this line?"

7. When students respond, "He's really poor. Sangmin must be what the poor people are called," or something of that nature, record the inference in the outer ring. As the story continues, the character of Song-ho becomes increasingly clear to students. I try to use three different colors on the chart to emphasize the different levels.

8. After completing the story, ask students to write a paragraph defining Song-ho's character. Students usually complete the paragraph with ease after this lesson.

Reading Workshop Link: *As students read on their own, have them draw three concentric circles for one of the characters in their journal. Have them fill this out as they read. (See Graphic Organizer 5, page 57, for the template.)*

Using Picture Books to Teach Comprehension Strategies

Lesson 13:
Scaffolding Making Inferences to Compare and Contrast Characters

Beatrice's Goat
Author: Page McBrier
Illustrator: Lori Lohstoeter
Simon & Schuster, 2001

Learning objective:
Students will compare/contrast two characters from different stories by making inferences.

Comparing and contrasting characters can be a challenge for many students because it calls on a variety of skills. Students need to process character descriptions, make inferences about similarities and differences between the characters, and then synthesize all this information to make evaluations. This requires higher-level thinking skills and true understanding of what one reads.

The humanitarian organization Heifer International promotes *Beatrice's Goat* to provide information on this important charity. This charity provides the gift of farm animals to poor families in developing countries. A gift of this sort provides a family with increased financial security and self-sufficiency. This national best seller tells about young Beatrice who lives with her large family on a banana plantation in Uganda. Beatrice longs to go to school. She walks by the local school, hoping that one day she may be able to attend. Fortunately, Heifer International grants a pregnant goat named Mugisa to Beatrice's family. Mugisa gives birth to twins, one of which is sold, allowing Beatrice to purchase the uniform necessary to enroll at school. The family begins its own herd, and the story ends on a note of joy and hope.

Materials
1 or more copies of *The Royal Bee*
The character chart created for Song-ho in the previous lesson
1 or more copies of *Beatrice's Goat*
Copies of Graphic Organizer 5: Targeting Character Inferences, page 57

What to Do

1. Display *Beatrice's Goat* in the reading area. With *The Royal Bee* nearby, introduce *Beatrice's Goat*.

2. Call attention to the character graphic organizer about Song-Ho posted on the wall.

3. Ask students to share how they determined Song-ho's character in this previous activity. Discuss. Listen for solid definitions of inferring and a firm understanding of the lesson's process.

4. Restate the purpose of each circle in the wheel. The center is for the character's name. Say, "In the next circle out, we record what the author says about the character in the book and what the character says and does. In the outer circle, we will make our inferences by using this information from the book and our own background knowledge."

5. Provide each student with Graphic Organizer 5 and a clipboard. Say, "Put the name of Beatrice into the middle circle. She is the character we will focus on in this story. As I read, you may fill out the second circle. Listen for what the character says and does and write it down there. At the end of the story, we will make some inferences about Beatrice in the outer ring."

6. Read the story to students, pausing at each page for students to record words and actions. Some common statements are:

* Beatrice lives in a new house made of mud. She must be poor or she lives in a very different place.
* She works all day in the fields and watches younger children. There is no money. She must work to help her mother survive.
* Beatrice watches the school children from afar and wishes to attend school, too. Maybe she worries about getting an education. She wants to learn to read and be like other kids.
* Beatrice has no money for a uniform. She can't go to school without it.
* Beatrice works harder than ever preparing for the family's new gift of a goat. She is responsible. She worries about her family and wants the best for them.
* Beatrice makes sure Mugisa the goat has extra grass and water. She is kind and compassionate.

7. At the end of the story, I make sure to read the afterword by Hillary Rodham Clinton to provide additional information.

8. Ask students to compare their second circle on the graphic organizer with that of a partner.

9. Have partners fill in their inferences in the outer circle and discuss each of them.

10. Send students to their seats to write a paragraph on the back of the graphic organizer. The paragraph should tell about three similarities between Song-ho and Beatrice, and three differences.

Using Picture Books to Teach Comprehension Strategies

Secret Ingredient: You can use this story as the basis for a writing prompt. Ask students to tell about a time they had to work to get something they really wanted. What did they do? Were they successful? Was it worth it? For younger students, use *Beatrice's Goat* to teach sequencing.

Lesson 14:
Scaffolding Making Inferences to Determine the Author's Meaning

Sister Anne's Hands
Author: Marybeth Lorbiecki
Illustrator: Wendy Popp
Dial Books, 1998.

Learning objective:
Students will determine author's meaning or theme by making inferences about plot and characters.

I was immediately drawn to *Sister Anne's Hands* when I spotted it at my local bookstore. This book challenges students to use the strategy of making inferences to determine theme or author's message. The author does not plainly state the grave conflict of intolerance in the story, but rather develops the concept through the conversation of characters and events. The beautiful pastel illustrations are contemplative and gentle. And yet within these pictures, something as ugly as racism lurks.

The setting is a Catholic school in the mid-1960s. One day, 7-year-old Anna overhears her parents whispering about the new teacher. She hears Dad say, "I don't know how a woman of her color is going to survive." This utterly confuses young Anna and she finds herself worrying about the new school year and her new teacher. The night before her first day, she dreams her new teacher could be any color of the rainbow.

When she meets Sister Anne, the nun who has come to be her teacher, Anna is surprised to see she is African American. At first, Anna hides from her teacher and refuses to touch her. Some students leave the class, but Anna soon discovers her fears were unfounded as she befriends her new teacher. Sister

Anne takes Anna and her classmates outside to draw and teaches them all kinds of amazing new things. She has an entertaining way of teaching math and uses funny voices when reading stories. Everything is like the Garden of Eden, until a paper airplane flies through the classroom and hits Sister Anne. On it is a racist message. Sister Anne's peaceful and loving response to this prejudice is triumphant and well worth a discussion in the classroom.

Materials

1 or more copies of *Sister Anne's Hands*
Butcher paper chart copied from page 63
Copies of Graphic Organizer 6: Using Inferences to Determine Theme, page 63

What to Do

1. Gather students to the reading carpet. Hold up *Sister Anne's Hands*, showing the cover and saying, "Do you ever wonder why authors make books?" Allow time for student response, listening for the suggestion that authors make books to teach life lessons.

2. Say, "Today we will use the strategy of making inferences to determine the theme of a book. The theme is an author's life message to the reader. Sometimes I call life messages 'an author's secret message to kids' because writers rarely come right out and tell readers a book's theme. They only show us the theme through characters and events in the story. By thinking about what is happening in the story, we can eventually determine why the author wrote the book for us. We figure out the life message that we are supposed to learn."

3. Introduce *Sister Anne's Hands*.

4. Point out the butcher paper posted nearby. (See right.)

5. Say to students, "In the first column we will simply record a quote from the book that says something about what a character says or does, or an important event."
Write "Quote" and "Page Number" at the top of the column.

Name _____ **Graphic Organizer 6**

Using Inferences to Determine Theme

Book _____ Author _____

Quote and Page Number	Our Inferences	Author's Message

Theme Statement
_____
_____
_____
_____

Using Picture Books to Teach Comprehension Strategies

Name _____

Using Inferences to Determine Theme

Book _____ Author _____

Quote and Page Number	Our Inferences	Author's Message

Theme Statement

_____

_____

_____

_____

6. Say, "In the second column we will record our inference about the quote." Title this column "Our Inferences."

7. Say, "The last column is an important one. This is where we will use our inferences and quotes to find out the author's secret message, meaning, or theme."

8. Begin reading. Occasionally stop and record a quote. Ask students what they can infer from the quote and what the author means by it. You may have to model this at first, but eventually students usually become quite proficient at it.

9. At the end of the story, draw students' attention to the third column and discuss comments to determine author's meaning. Together, create a theme statement for this book. Possible themes: *Racism isn't fair. People lose out on opportunities when they judge others by their skin color. Prejudice keeps people from doing what they want to do with their life.* Record the theme statement on the butcher paper.

Reading Workshop Link: *As students read individually, pass out Graphic Organizer 6 (page 63) and ask them to practice this lesson individually. I like to assign a basal story for my students to read individually. I make sure to find one with a strong life message.*

Secret Ingredient: For writing workshop, ask students about a time they solved a serious problem in a peaceful way. Allow writing time and then invite students to share their stories.

Name _____   **Graphic Organizer 6**

Using Inferences to Determine Theme

Book _____   Author _____

Quote and Page Number	Our Inferences	Author's Message
When she reached out to touch my cheek, I dodged her hand as if it were hot.	*She's afraid of Sister Anne because her skin is different, probably from what her parents said the night before. She's not sure it will be okay.*	*The author shows us what people do when they are afraid of other people. Sometimes we judge people before we get to really know them.*

Other Books to Teach the Strategy of Making Inferences

On pages 136–141 in the Appendix, I've included an author study of Chris Van Allsburg's books that is great for teaching students to make inferences.

Probuditi!, by Chris Van Allsburg

Moses: When Harriet Tubman Led Her People to Freedom, by Carole Boston Weatherford

Where Are You Going Manyoni?, by Catherine Stock

The Raft, by Jim LaMarche

Knots on a Counting Rope, by Bill Martin, Jr., and John Archambault

Old Crump, by Laurie Lawlor

Weslandia, by Paul Fleischman

The Little Match Girl, by Jerry Pinkney

How Many Days to America?, by Eve Bunting

The Gardener, by Sarah Stewart

George and Martha, by James Marshall

Gleam and Glow, by Eve Bunting (or for any other strategy)

Encounter, by Jane Yolen

The Wall, by Eve Bunting

June 29, 1999, by David Wiesner (or any of his other books)

Chapter 4

Making Predictions

"Mrs. Zimny!" gasped Brian. "Did you remember to put out the lunch count?" I became instantly rattled by this innocent question. It wasn't a bad question; it just came right in the middle of a lesson that I had spent hours planning. I had been excited to introduce a series of reading lessons on types of forests to support our new physical science unit. After spending ample time in the library, I had discovered an

Using Picture Books to Teach Comprehension Strategies

absolutely beautiful book on rain forests. Full of vibrant photographs, the book focused on the research of tree canopy scientist Dr. Nalini Nadkarni. I thought my students would love it.

I decided to ignore Brian's question and continue reading to my students. But after a few sentences I heard Alyssa say, "What time is the assembly? Shouldn't we be going?" I let out a sigh and put the book down. They just weren't into it. Looking around the reading carpet, I saw my students in various stages of falling asleep. Dutifully, they clutched their clipboards where I had asked them to record facts as I read, but their involvement was forced. It wasn't the book. It was the lesson. Despite the high-interest topic and great book, the activity was boring. I knew I had to get them personally involved.

Making Predictions: A Definition

When a reader makes predictions, he or she uses inferences, questions, and prior knowledge to determine what will happen (Harvey & Goudvis, 2007). Many strategies are synthesized into one. Michael Pressley, a reading researcher, writes that solid instruction "demands that readers make predictions as they read, with predicting always requiring that readers relate what they have encountered in the text with what they already know in order to gauge what happens next" (Pressley, 2006). When we start talking about what happens next, our curiosity is heightened and we become emotionally invested in the text. Making predictions during reading is one way to help students become active readers.

Selecting Picture Books to Support Prediction Strategy Instruction

Here are some questions to ask as you choose books for teaching the strategy of making predictions.

- Does the text present unfamiliar vocabulary, giving students the opportunity to predict meaning using context clues?
- If it's a narrative text, will the book's ending and format be unfamiliar to students, encouraging them to make predictions?
- Does the book present a problem that could be solved in a variety of ways?
- Does the book contain foreshadowing to foster making predictions?
- Are the illustrations compelling and detailed to prompt predictions?

Lesson 15:
Making Predictions With Informational Text

Rain Forest
Author: Jinny Johnson with Dr. Nalini Nadkarni
Houghton Mifflin, 2006

Learning objective:
Students will make predictions about topics while reading an informational text.

I first saw *Rain Forest* in a box of new books for our school's Scholastic Book Fair. Drawn in by the cover, I quickly grabbed it and found a quiet place to gaze at the phenomenal pictures. The pages show mist-covered mountains, thundering rivers, the levels of the rain forest, tribal villages, maps, and exotic animals, birds, and flowers. The book is organized into three tabbed sections titled Into the Forest, Up in the Trees, and Life at the Top. The organized sections keep the abundance of color, photos, and text from overwhelming the reader.

Initially I used the book for gathering facts in our science unit, but I eventually realized *Rain Forest* becomes more powerful when used for modeling reading strategies. Many students struggle with making predictions about topics in informational text, particularly when looking to answer research questions. In my classroom, *Rain Forest* became an excellent book for modeling prediction strategies in nonfiction.

Materials
1 or more copies of *Rain Forest*
Large piece of butcher paper with a copy of *Rain Forest's* cover posted at the top
1 sticky note for each student
Copies of Graphic Organizer 7: The Why Question, page 69 (optional)

What to Do

1. Gather students to the reading area and introduce *Rain Forest*.

2. As children watch, draw the graphic organizer shown on the next page onto the butcher paper that you've posted on the wall.

3. Open to the section titled Into the Forest. Say, "Good readers of nonfiction use predictions to help them understand the facts in the text. Sometimes asking a why question before we read and then predicting an answer can help us to remember better. It also helps us to be more involved in our reading. Watch me as I explore this beautiful book and predict what will happen based on some of the information presented."

The Why Question

Book _____   Author _____

Why	My Prediction	Answer

4. Turn to the page with the subtitle Down in the Roots. Don't read the text, but draw students' attention to the pictures.

ME: Wow, kids. Look at this picture [picture of woman measuring a three-foot flower bloom]. I am wondering about this. Why would they include a picture of a flower in this section?

KRISTIN: Maybe the flowers need the tree roots.

ALEX: Maybe the flowers are helping the trees in some way. Like maybe they help the tree roots.

ME: Hmm. Well, I am going to write a why question about this on the chart. [I write, "Why is this flower in the section called Down in the Roots?"] Now, in the second column I am going to make a prediction about the answer. What should I write?

KRISTIN: Put "I think the flower helps the tree in some way."

ALEX: I would put that the flower is just part of the forest floor. Down in the Roots means what is on the forest floor.

ME: I think I'll write "The flower is part of the forest floor and may help the tree in some way." [Record in second column.]

Name _____   **Graphic Organizer 7**

The Why Question

Book _____   Author _____

Why	My Prediction	Answer
Why is there a weird flower in this section?	*The flower needs the tree roots.*	*The author said the forest floor is too dark for flowers, but this one can still grow there. It smells like rotting meat and attracts good bugs.*
Why are the gorillas sitting together? Do they live there? Why are they important?	*They live there because they can hide from people and get lots of food.*	*Gorillas are one of the largest animals that live on the forest floor. A male gorilla can be over 5-feet tall. They live in family groups in only two small areas in central Africa.*
Why are the tarantulas floating on the river?	*Tarantulas can swim to safety.*	*The Amazon River rises and floods the land. Animals learn to cope until the river goes back down. Two-thirds of all fresh water on our planet is in the Amazon River basin!*
Why are insects so important?	*The insects need to break down all the dying plant life.*	*Insects make up a miniature world on the forest floor. They work at eating up decaying plant and animal life to keep the forest "clean." Millions of army ants eat everything in their path while millipedes can grow up to a foot long.*
Why do people still live there?	*Maybe people live there because they're poor. Maybe they like it.*	*The book doesn't mention the people living in the rainforest now, but we know they do because of the picture with the kids in a boat.*
Why did they build those funny looking pyramids?	*The mysterious buildings are part of some past civilization.*	*Great temples and palaces can be found in Central America. The Mayans built them during the peak of their civilization, A.D. 250–900. One of the temples, called the Temple of the Grand Jaguar, was built in A.D. 700 and stands higher than 148 feet. No one knows why the ancient civilization collapsed.]*

5. Read the page with students. In the third column record the answer to the why question.

ME: What should I record for the answer?

KRISTIN: It's one of the only flowers that grow on the forest floor. Things are too dark.

ALEX: Yeah, the author is saying it's mostly dead and decaying stuff on the forest floor because the trees block the light. For some reason this flower grows and attracts insects for pollination.

KRISTIN: It's gross that it smells like rotting meat. That's probably how it attracts the bugs to help the trees.

I record the answer "It attracts insects that help the trees" from the text on our chart.

6. Continue to turn the pages and write why questions and predictions as you skim. Read the text to fill in the last column. Check for accuracy of predictions.

7. Turn to the section titled Up in the Trees and skim each page with students. Students record their own why question for this section on a sticky note. Call them up to share their questions and post them in the first column of the butcher paper. Together, predict answers to some of the questions. Read the section to see if the why questions are answered.

8. For more practice, hand out Graphic Organizer 7: The Why Question. Go over the third section of the book titled, Life at the Top, and have students fill out their papers as you go.

> **Reading Workshop Link:** *As students read on their own, ask them to use the graphic organizer or simply copy it into their Reading Journals to fill out and use to increase understanding. This can also be practiced in other content areas.*

Secret Ingredient: Use *Rain Forest* to teach glossary or index skills.

Lesson 16:
Modeling the Importance of Making Predictions to Understand Text

The Snow Princess
Author and Illustrator: Ruth Sanderson
Little, Brown, 2004

Learning objective:
Students will make predictions together to practice this reading strategy.

In this lesson, students make predictions about the outcome of a story.

I purchased *The Snow Princess* for the sole purpose of modeling prediction. I needed a book that none of my students had read. The best thing was simply to buy an obscure book that couldn't be found in the school library. *The Snow Princess* turned out to be a strong book for teaching prediction because it follows the fairy tale format, provides foreshadowing in the text and pictures, and presents a conflict that could be resolved in several possible ways. Also, the illustrations are phenomenal. Based on a Russian opera, the book possesses lots of drama. The plot keeps students riveted.

Snow Princess is born to Father Frost and Mother Spring. She lives an uncomplicated life, conjuring up little snowstorms and impressing her doting parents. Finally she reaches womanhood and decides she needs a little excitement. She begs her parents to let her leave their icy home so she can visit other parts of the world. They grudgingly agree, but her father tells her she will only be safe as long as the love of a man never enters her heart. If it does, Snow Princess will face certain death.

In her travels, *Snow Princess* finds a human family and eventually falls in love with the oldest son, Sergei. She knows she will die, so she runs away. Of course, she is unable to stay away and the love of a man obscures her sense of reason. When she returns, she learns that Sergei is lost in a terrible storm that she had conjured up during her deep depression. She finds him, and they marry after a somewhat encouraging visit from Mother Spring, who informs her daughter that she will certainly die, but only after leading a long human life.

Materials

1 or more copies of *The Snow Princess*
Large piece of butcher paper with a copy of the book's cover attached to the center
1 piece of drawing paper for each group of students
Markers for each team

What to Do

1. Gather students on the reading carpet and introduce *The Snow Princess*.

2. Point out the butcher paper posted behind you and say, "Today we are learning about how good readers make predictions when they read. When we make a prediction, we take clues from the book to think about what may happen next. While making predictions, good readers are really inferring. They combine what they already know about the story and look for author clues as to how the story may end."

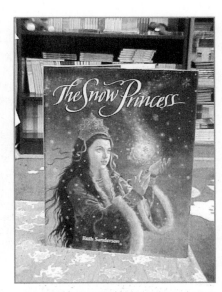

3. Say, "As I read, look for clues to a possible ending. Make sure you look at the pictures as well as listen to the text."

Our lesson book on display.

4. Begin to read the story, allowing students to comment and discuss as they go. Listen to what they notice. When you hear predictions, stop and ask students what their predictions are based on, such as foreshadowing in the text or picture clues. One of the most important questions you can ask right now is, "Why do you think so?"

5. Stop on the page where poor Snow Princess must decide whether to return to Sergei. She curls up into a snowstorm and states, "My heart is cold." At this point, I send groups of three or four students back to their seats with a paper and markers. They are told to predict an ending using clues in the text and the pictures. The team draws what they think the last page of the book looks like and writes out its prediction with two supporting details from the text.

6. Circulate and listen to student conversations. I listen for predictions being made, discussions over possibilities, and textual support for predictions. The fact that Snow Princess will die if she returns to Sergei presents students with an extra challenge in determining a possible ending.

7. Gather students back to the reading carpet. When it is time to come back to the carpet, students practically run. They cannot wait to hear whether their prediction matches the ending.

8. Allow each group to present its prediction and the two details that support it. As they share, post the papers on the chart to document learning.

9. Before you read the ending, add more suspense by leaning toward them and saying, "You guys need to prepare yourselves . . . ! Are you ready?"

10. Read the ending and allow time to discuss their responses.

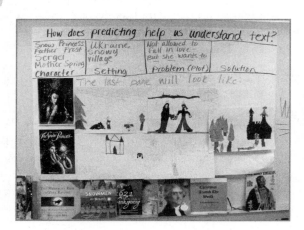

Our class chart showing how to use story elements to predict story outcome.

Students inevitably develop fairy-tale predictions and usually predict that Father Frost or Mother Spring will rescue their daughter. Of course, as we read it, we figure out that Snow Princess becomes human and thus, must succumb to death after a long, happy life, as we all do.

Reading Workshop Link: *Send students to their Reading Journals to write this reflection: How did you make predictions during the reading of* The Snow Princess? *What would you tell a new student about how to use the predicting strategy?*

Secret Ingredient: Watch your students and see if they notice how Snow Princess's appearance changes with each page. Her face gains more color and she becomes more like a human as the story progresses.

Using Picture Books to Teach Comprehension Strategies

Lesson 17:
Extra Practice Lesson on Making Predictions

Santa's Snow Cat
Author: Sue Stainton
Illustrator: Anne Mortimer
HarperCollins, 2001

I post predictions from teams and individual students on the chart.

Because I teach the prediction strategy right before winter break, I use stories that fit the holiday atmosphere in my classroom. The pictures in *Santa's Snow Cat* are festive and the writing positively sparkles with description, making it a powerful addition to a trait writing lesson on word choice, too. I use it to reinforce the strategy of making predictions while using the lesson template of *The Snow Princess*.

In this tale, Snow Cat lives with Santa in the beautiful North Pole. One night, she slips into Santa's pocket, blending in with the thick white fur of his coat. It happens to be Christmas Eve and she ends up flying through the sky on the most magical night of the year.

Stainton's beautiful language just doesn't stop. She loads the text with personification. Lemon Moon and North Wind become wonderful characters as she gives them human traits and emotions. Unfortunately, the happy tale takes a scary turn when the curious Snow Cat leans out too far and ends up falling into the hustle and bustle of New York City. (I like to see if my kids can infer this by the picture of the Empire State Building.) Snow Cat searches and searches for Santa, to no avail. She ends up entering a strange home and curling up under the tree, where, of course, Santa finds her.

I use this text just as I use *The Snow Princess*. I stop reading about midway and the teams are sent back to discuss a prediction. When we meet on the carpet again, we go over our predictions. I am vigilant at this point to ensure they are supporting their predictions with details from the text. Just stating a prediction is not enough. Sometimes before sending students to work, I provide each student with a sticky note to record an individual prediction with supporting details. In this way, I can check for individual understanding.

This text is fairly simple, but there is one important note. The book was published just months prior to 9/11. In the book, just before finding his beloved cat, Santa lands on the Twin Towers, which Stainton refers to as "the tallest of tall buildings." The picture shows Santa climbing the Twin Towers, struggling to find his precious pet. You'll need to assess whether this book is appropriate for your class.

A close-up of
one student's work.

Secret Ingredient: I use this book to teach word choice, personification, and irony. I also discuss the word "bittersweet" with my students. The book is perfect for teaching about descriptive language in writing workshop.

Lesson 18:
Using Storyboards to Scaffold Making Accurate Predictions

Minty
Author: Alan Schroeder
Illustrator: Jerry Pinkney
Puffin Books, 1996

Learning objective:
Students will practice making accurate predictions with the use of a storyboard.

Minty, a Coretta Scott King Award recipient, has mature content and requires some historical context. I personally wouldn't dip below fourth grade with this one. I use it to directly teach and scaffold making predictions, primarily because the author uses foreshadowing to hint at future events. Story elements such as conflict and character development also make this book a powerful tool for teaching the predicting strategy. *Minty* explores the important themes of freedom and the ugliness of slavery, making it a book that can foster deep discussion and reflection.

Minty, or Araminta, was the cradle name of Harriet Tubman. This book is a fictionalized account of her childhood, although all of the major events and ideas are fact. Young Minty lives a miserable life on the Brodas plantation, where she is subjected to a life of hard work and constant humiliation. She endures the cruelty of Mrs. Brodas, the wife of the plantation owner, who mercilessly burns her only toy. She works the entire day in sweltering heat and is finally assigned the task of going into a frightening river to pull in muskrat traps. As it turns out, Minty cannot bear the imprisonment of the small creatures, and she releases them. Unfortunately, an overseer witnesses this and Mrs. Brodas has her beaten. But Minty's incredible spirit cannot be broken. One night, she senses her chance to escape. A saddled horse has been left outside and she approaches the horse, thinking she can get away. As it turns out, she hesitates for a moment and her chance is lost.

Materials

1 or more copies of *Minty*

Copies of the Graphic Organizer 8: Storyboard Prediction, page 78

What to Do

1. Gather students on the carpet and introduce *Minty*.

2. Say, "We have been talking about how good readers make predictions as they read. Yesterday we worked on making predictions about possible solutions to the story conflict based on some clue in a story. Today, I'd like to talk about how good readers make predictions about other story elements as well."

3. Point out the graphic organizer. Say, "The first box here is labeled Character. Then we have Problem and Setting. Good readers can make predictions about all of these story elements. We will use this storyboard to help us keep on track as we read *Minty*."

4. Begin reading the book. I don't tell students the main character is Harriet Tubman at first. It is perfectly fine for students with prior knowledge to figure this out as you read, but knowing that the book is about Tubman may interfere with predictions in the beginning.

5. Read up until the point where Minty sets the muskrats free from the river cages.

6. Turn to the chart and have students help fill it out. In each box, write what they have learned so far in the story.

ME: Here we will write up some notes about Minty, the main character. What do we know about her so far?

D.J.: She is a slave and she has a mean boss. She wants to run away.

ME: OK. What is her personality like? What have you inferred?

KATE: She wants to be free. She doesn't always obey the rules.

JAMES: Sometimes she tries to fight back, like when Mrs. Brodas burned her doll, Esther.

D.J.: Yeah. She lets the muskrats go even though she's probably going to get in trouble for it.

Name _____   **Graphic Organizer 8**

Storyboard Prediction

Book _____   Author _____

Character	I predict the character will
	_____
	_____
	_____
	_____
	_____

Problem	I predict the problem will be resolved by
	_____
	_____
	_____
	_____
	_____

Setting	I predict the setting may change
	_____
	_____
	_____
	_____
	_____

ME: She lets the muskrats go. What does that tell you about her personality?

D.J.:   She disobeys. She's going to get in trouble again and she doesn't even care.

KATE: I think it means that she hates to see anything caught. She feels bad for the animals so she lets them go. I don't blame her.

ME: So this means she is compassionate?

KATE: Yes. She cares about suffering animals. She can't stand to see them suffer so she rescues them.

7.   After filling in the Character box, I direct students' attention to the lined area next to the box and ask for predictions about the character.

ME: You did a great job finding some clues about Minty's personality. Let's move over to this area and write a prediction about the main character. For example, what will she do next? What will happen to her?

D.J: She's going to get in trouble again. She got in trouble last time she disobeyed.

JAMES: Yeah, she keeps getting caught. She also told her mom she would run away. If she runs away, she'd better figure out how not to get caught. Maybe they would kill her.

KATE: She can't run away right now. She's only eight and she always gets caught. I think she is going to learn to do things without getting caught. Maybe she will get away, but she can't right now.

D.J: But maybe she'll run away because she doesn't want to get in trouble.

ME: So what should I write?

Name _____   **Graphic Organizer 8**

Storyboard Prediction

Book ___Minty_____   Author ___Alan Schroeder_____

Character	I predict the character will
Minty disobeys. She is compassionate.	get in trouble for disobeying. She may run away.

D.J: Write that she'll run away before she gets in trouble.

KATE: I don't know. Maybe someone is going to help her. Like Amanda. I think Amanda or someone is going to come get her.

ME: [recording what is said] Tell me how you know this. We need to write two supports for our prediction.

JAMES: She told her mom she was going to run away.

D.J: She's a fighter, too. She tried to fight Mrs. Brodas. I don't think she'll obey the rules at all.

KATE: Also, she sets the muskrats free. I think that's important. She hates to see things not free.

8. Continue to fill out the chart in this manner. Finish reading the book and return to the chart to discuss the accuracy of students' predictions.

Reading Workshop Link: *Give students copies of Graphic Organizer 8 on page 78 to fill out as they read their own books. Watch for challenged students. This graphic organizer can be overwhelming because it covers several elements of story. Cutting the paper into strips and working on one element at a time could help.*

Note: This book also works well in the lesson used for *The Snow Princess*. I read up to the point where Minty is about to steal a horse and then send groups back to their seats to predict an ending. When students come back to the carpet, we discuss their predictions. It helps to write them on chart paper and also to record the reasons for the predictions. Then I finish reading and children view the last page of the book: a dismal Minty lying on the floor, crying to herself while the rest of her family sleeps soundly around her. Many of the children will be surprised to see that she does not leave, but I remind them that the text told us she was only 8. How can an 8-year-old overcome such a thing as slavery?

At this point, I tell children who Minty really is. Some children will recognize this famous woman. I give a little history, and then we talk about clues in the story about how Minty will one day be "the Moses of her people." I am always fascinated by the ability of fourth graders to be able to really pull information from the text. Usually they tell me that her father had taught her skills for running away. I will never forget one class that had said, "We know she comes back to rescue others because of the muskrats. She let them go because she couldn't bear to see anything not free." That's a goose bump moment!

Secret Ingredient: I use *Minty* for teaching descriptive language. The part where she is about to steal the horse also works well for lessons on building tension or suspense in writing.

Lesson 19:
Making Predictions to Determine an Author's Meaning

The Rag Coat
Author and Illustrator: Lauren Mills
Little, Brown, 1991

Learning objective:
Students will practice making accurate predictions continuously throughout the reading of a text to determine an author's theme.

Because of the conflict presented in it, *The Rag Coat* is a great book to use for assessing students' ability to make predictions. This is a tearjerker tale set in Appalachian mining country. Minna, the main character, is an impoverished girl who longs to attend school. Her father, a miner, is dying of black lung disease. Minna is finally allowed to attend her local school, but when winter comes, this joyful possibility ends abruptly because she cannot afford to buy a winter coat. Then her father succumbs to his illness and dies.

Students remain "eye to eye" when working on a task to foster discussion and active involvement.

One day, the local women gather at her home and quilt a coat just for her by using their leftover scraps. Minna is thrilled. She can now attend school, anticipating the fun and happiness that she had before. However, on her first day, insensitive classmates meet Minna in the schoolyard and mock the beloved coat. Minna runs away and hides in the woods. The children naughtily tell the teacher that Minna was not feeling well.

Prediction and Meaning

Book _____ Author _____

Prediction	Reason for Prediction	Outcome of the Prediction	Possible Meaning

Using Picture Books to Teach Comprehension Strategies

Minna returns to school and shows the children her coat, explaining that each quilt square has some sort of memory within it. Her classmates recognize their own memories in her quilted coat, as it was their mothers who had made the coat. Minna especially treasures the little gray patch, made from her father's mining jacket. I always finish this book with a lump in my throat.

Materials

1 or more copies of *The Rag Coat*
Copies of Graphic Organizer 9: Prediction and Meaning, page 82
Chart paper with large drawing of the graphic organizer

What to Do

1. Gather students to the reading area and introduce *The Rag Coat*.

2. Point out the chart paper posted nearby and tell students that today they will be making predictions while reading a story.

3. Say, "As we read, quotes and pictures from the book may help us make some predictions. Good readers make predictions while they read because it helps them become more involved in the story. Predictions can also help readers determine the author's meaning. When I stop reading at certain places, share a prediction, if you have one."

4. Read the book and stop where Minna tells Mrs. Miller that she can't go to school.

5. Ask students whether they have any predictions and write them in the first column. Record reasons for the predictions in the second column. This is an important step because it teaches students to use text to support ideas.

6. Read up to the part where Minna adds a patch from her father's mining jacket to the coat.

7. Fill in the third column in the first row by asking students to share the actual outcome of the prediction. I like to push it further in the last column and ask them what the outcome tells us about the story or the author's meaning. Remind students that predictions are used to help us determine the meaning of a story.

8. Read the next page, which describes the night before Minna wears her new coat to school. Stop and begin to fill out the second row with students, asking what they think will happen when Minna wears the coat to school. Record thoughts and supporting details.

9. Read up to where Minna runs away from school because of the teasing. Finish the second row, asking what actually happened and what it tells us about the characters or the meaning of the book. (See Graphic Organizer 9, below.)

10. Read the part where Minna sits in the woods and decides to return to school. Begin to fill out the third row, asking how she will solve her problem. Once again, students should support predictions with evidence from the text.

11. Read the rest of the book. Check predictions and accuracy by filling out the rest of the third row.

12. Come to a class consensus about why the author wrote the book. What is the message she wants her readers to know? Remind students that this is called a story's theme.

Name _____ **Graphic Organizer 9**

Prediction and Meaning

Book _____ Author _____

Prediction	Reason for Prediction	Outcome of the Prediction	Possible Meaning
They will take the blanket and make it into a coat to help Minna.	*Picture of Minna quilting with two mothers. They look like they care about her. The blanket is called "Joseph's Coat."*	*They didn't use the blanket. They made the coat just for Minna.*	*The women are kind. They care about Minna. Even though they're also poor, they still help each other.*
She's going to wear it to school for Sharing Day. The kids will want to touch it. They might try to take it from her.	*They all wanted to touch the new doll Lottie brought. They are excited when someone gets a new thing. They might take the coat because the kids are kind of mean. One boy called her "stupid."*	*Minna wears it to school and the kids hate it. They tease her and call her "Rag Coat." She runs away.*	*Kids can be mean to other kids. They didn't like it because it was different. They made her feel like she didn't belong.*
She's going to go back to school and tell about the coat during her sharing time. She's going to show them the patch from her dad's mining coat. Then the kids will understand how special it is.	*She remembers what her dad says about people needing people. She doesn't want to let her father down. She doesn't care what the kids say because the coat makes her feel like her dad is hugging her.*	*She goes back to school and shares the patches from the kids' mothers. Each child in the class finds a patch that came from his or her own home and recalls a memory. They tell Minna her coat is the warmest of all.*	*It shows that people need people. It shows kids can be accepting of people once they know more about them.*

Using Picture Books to Teach Comprehension Strategies

Secret Ingredient: Use *The Rag Coat* as a writing workshop activity on memoirs. Give students brown lunch bags and ask them to bring in something that represents a special memory to them. Students can write about the special memory as a memoir during writing workshop and then share with the whole class.

Other Books to Teach the Strategy of Making Predictions

The Dragon Prince, by Laurence Yep

Almost to Freedom, by Vaunda Micheaux Nelson

Who's That Knocking on Christmas Eve, by Jan Brett

The Hungry Giant of the Tundra, retold by Teri Sloat

White Water, by Jonathan London and Aaron London

The Spider Weaver, by Margaret Musgrove

The Magic Nesting Doll, by Jacqueline K. Ogburn

Eagle Boy, retold by Richard Lee Vaughan

Swamp Angel, by Anne Isaacs

The Lady & The Lion, retold by Laurel Long and Jacqueline K. Ogburn

The Singing Man, by Angela Shelf Medearis

The Well at the End of the World, by Robert San Souci

Chapter 5

Determining Importance

Sitting like perfect rows of soldiers, my fourth graders squirmed with delight. I was excited, too. Shirley, a principal at a neighboring school, had come to visit us. I was thrilled to have this excellent mentor and friend all to myself for the morning. Sitting in a chair in the back of the room, she radiated kindness to every child in the classroom. With recess just minutes away, I began to share the book *Feathers and Fools* by Mem Fox. I couldn't wait for my students to hear the important message of peace in this book about a war started by foolishness. But teaching is heavy with humbling surprises, and before I could get to the third page, my students were giggling into their hands. "Stop giggling," I muttered, looking nervously back at our visitor. "This is a serious story." With each passing page, the giggling grew louder. By the time the peacocks and swans were shooting each other with sharpened feathers, my students could hardly contain outright laughter. I looked back at Shirley in dismay only to find her giggling as well.

As students ran out for recess, Shirley and I had time to sit and talk. I jokingly told her I thought my students were little monsters to laugh at the story, but she dabbed the tears from chuckling out of her eyes and said, "You should have seen your face. I know you were expecting a different reaction, Joanne. Yes, the kids missed the point of the story, but it is a special story that takes a special approach and now you know. Anyway, they understood part of it. They laughed because the birds were fighting over something ridiculous. They just couldn't determine which ideas in the story were important."

Determining Importance: A Definition

Determining the importance of ideas in text is essential to understanding an author's purpose. As students gain proficiency with this reading strategy, they become adept at determining the theme or main idea, summarizing, and evaluating what they read. Keene and Zimmermann (1998) write, "Determining importance means revealing that which may be denied or ignored—those key themes and ideas that hide beneath the surface and may go unnoticed if we don't bring them to our conscious attention" (p. 93). They go on to add that determining importance also includes determining what is not important. When modeling and scaffolding this strategy, I make sure my students have ample access to fiction as well as nonfiction. As the lessons in this chapter will show, determining importance in these two genres sometimes requires different skills

Selecting Picture Books to Support Determining Importance Strategy Instruction

Here are some questions to ask as you choose books for teaching the strategy of determining importance.

♦ Do action and speech patterns clearly portray character traits?

♦ If the book is a biographical picture book, can the five W's be used?

♦ Does the book contain compelling words and details that lead to theme?

♦ Does the story present a series of steps to resolve a problem?

♦ Is there a life message or theme hidden within the pages?

♦ Do nonfiction books use text features such as maps, diagrams, bolded words, and subtitles to present important information?

Lesson 20:
Modeling Rising/Falling Action to Determine Importance

Feathers and Fools
Author: Mem Fox
Illustrator: Nicholas Wilton
Harcourt Brace, 1989

Learning objective:
Students will determine important ideas related to plot in a narrative by identifying essential parts of a story.

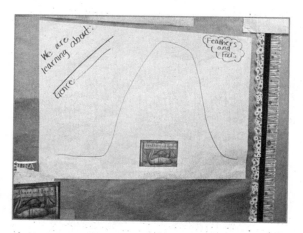

The beginning of our story mountain for *Feathers and Fools*.

Feathers and Fools is a beautifully illustrated allegory exploring the causes of war. The story begins on a peaceful pond, where peacocks and swans swim happily together. However, one day a peacock becomes suspicious of the swans, pointing out that swans possess the power to swim and fly. The peacocks become afraid of the swans and cry, "They may try to change our way of life!" The peacocks begin to make arrows out of old feathers, and tension on the pond increases. The swans notice the peacocks' hostile attitude and activity, and thus begin to make their own arrows.

One fateful day, a swan flies by with a twig in her beak for a nest. The peacocks see it, mistaking it for an arrow. They head to the pond and a fight ensues. Eventually, every bird is killed. The story ends with two eggs hatching . . . a peacock and a swan. They notice all the things they have in common and decide to become friends.

I love using this book to introduce determining importance in plot because it has clear rising and falling action. The essential parts of plot are: beginning, rising action, climax, falling action, ending, and resolution. This is what I like to call a "story mountain" for narrative writing.

Materials

1 or more copies of *Feathers and Fools*

Large piece of butcher paper with Graphic Organizer 10: Story Mountain, page 90, drawn on it

What to Do

1. I begin by creating a story mountain chart on the wall where students and I can read it together. (See Graphic Organizer 10, page 90.)

A completed story mountain for *Feathers and Fools*.

2. Introduce *Feathers and Fools* to students.

3. Say, "Narrative stories usually come with the same outline. There is a beginning, rising action, climax, falling action, ending, and a resolution. In the beginning of the story, the author normally presents the characters, the setting, and the conflict. We place this at the base of the mountain (on the left). Then we watch the action increase. The problem may get worse, and the story gets increasingly exciting. This is called the rising action (I label this on the chart). The top of the mountain is the climax, where we don't know how the story will turn out. The rising action comes to a peak and a huge event takes place—or an event where there is some kind of change. Then we have the falling action and finally the ending at the base of the mountain. The resolution is much different from an ending. The resolution tells us how the conflict was solved."

4. Label the story mountain graphic organizer with the important parts of the plot mentioned in Step 3.

5. Have students form groups of three or four. Tell each team which part of the plot they will be responsible for (beginning (character, setting, and conflict), rising action, climax, falling action, ending, and resolution).

Story Mountain

Book _____ Author _____

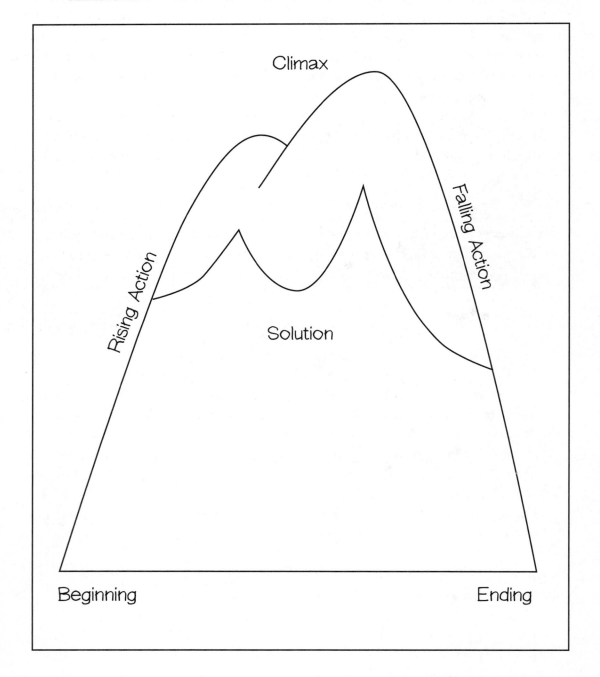

Climax

Falling Action

Rising Action

Solution

Beginning

Ending

6. Direct each team to listen for information regarding its part of the plot while you read. Say, "When we are done reading, you will go back to your table and draw a picture presenting your part of the plot. Then you will share your picture with the class."

7. Read the story and listen to students' comments as you go.

8. Send teams off to work on the tasks once you conclude the story. Circulate among students to check for understanding. In my own experience, I usually have to support students working on finding the climax of the story; the rising and falling action teams will need to know the climax in order to complete their tasks as well. Remember, this is an introduction, and your assistance during the activity is where a lot of teaching will be needed.

9. Gather together and allow groups to share, placing drawings on the chart as you go. As the plot is discussed, listen for insight into the meaning of the book, such as how prejudice can cause conflict. Remember, authors can have multiple meanings in stories. Be willing to listen to fresh insights from students.

Reading Workshop Link: *Pass out copies of Graphic Organizer 10 (page 90) or have students draw it in their reading journals. To check for understanding and provide practice, ask students to read a story in their reading basal or book of choice, filling out the organizer as they go.*

Lesson 21:
Determining Importance About Characters

Mufaro's Beautiful Daughters: An African Tale
Author and Illustrator: John Steptoe
Lothrop, Lee & Shepard Books, 1987

Learning objective:

Students will determine what is important about characters by reading
Mufaro's Beautiful Daughters and recording what characters do and say.

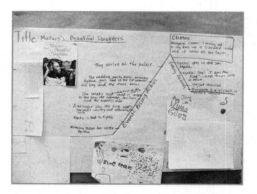

A story mountain for *Mufaro's Beautiful Daughters*.

Mufaro's Beautiful Daughters is the first picture book I ever used in the classroom and it remains one of my favorites. Years ago, as a first-year teacher, I purchased the book for its beautiful portrayal of the Zimbabwe region. I loved the story about inner beauty and the fascinating twists and turns in the plot. This marvelous book can be used to teach any reading strategy.

The story is about young Nyasha and her sister Manyara, daughters of the chieftain Mufaro. Nyasha lives a happy, peaceful life in her village. She tends a garden and is kind to all around her, even a tiny garden snake named Nyoka. The only upsetting thing in her life is Manyara. Manyara has a nasty attitude and continually hisses cruel remarks to her sister when their father is not around. One day, Mufaro hears that the prince in a neighboring village needs a wife. Mufaro decides to take his two daughters to see if the wealthy prince would marry one of them. In her greed, Manyara takes off the night before in order to get there first. Along the way, she refuses food to a child, scolds a wise woman, and encounters laughing trees and a headless man. When the rest of the tribe awakens, they find Manyara gone but decide to travel on without her. Nyasha responds kindly to the hungry child and the wise woman, and the enchanted trees along the way prophetically bow to her as she passes. When they reach the city,

Manyara hysterically runs toward them to warn everyone of an enormous monster in the prince's home. Nyasha bravely enters the palace and sees her little pet Nyoka on the throne. He praises her for her kind heart and turns into the handsome prince.

This story is perfect for teaching determining importance. The author gives us a hand by telling the readers that names are important in Africa. Mufaro means "happy man," Nyasha means "mercy," and Manyara means "ashamed."

Materials

1 or more copies of *Mufaro's Beautiful Daughters*
Large piece of butcher paper

What to Do

1. Before sharing this African folk tale, post butcher paper on the wall near the reading area. Label the chart Important Ideas About Characters. Underneath the title, draw three columns. Label the first column Mufaro, the second column Nyasha, and the third column Manyara.

Important Ideas About Characters		
Mufaro	Nyasha	Manyara

2. Gather students on the reading carpet and introduce *Mufaro's Beautiful Daughters*.

3. Read the dedication page, where the author explains the meanings of each name. Write the meanings next to the names on the chart.

4. Say, "Today we are learning how to determine important information about characters. As I read this book, let's listen for evidence that supports each character's name. Raise your hand when you think you hear something and we can record it on the chart."

5. Read the story. You will see the chart develop like the one on the next page.

Important Ideas About Characters		
Mufaro	**Nyasha**	**Manyara**
Happy Man. He has two beautiful daughters. He doesn't know they fight. He wants the best for his daughters.	*Mercy. She's beautiful. She says nice things to her sister. She sang as she worked. She is kind to the snake. She gives food to the child.*	*Ashamed. She's always in a bad temper. She thinks her father loves her sister best. She wants to be queen.*

6. Fill out the chart as you read. When finished, ask students to write a paragraph that compares and contrasts the two sisters. Remind them to include the important information about each character.

Using *Mufaro's Beautiful Daughters* to Scaffold Important Elements of Plot

This is a great book to use to reinforce the story mountain introduced in the *Feathers and Fools* lesson (see Graphic Organizer 10, page 90). I draw a mountain on a large chart. At the base on the left side, write Character/Setting/Conflict, explaining that these things are usually introduced early in a story. Up the left side of the mountain, we have the rising action, the top is the climax, and down the right side is the falling action. The base at the right side is the resolution. After reading the story, teams go off to illustrate one of these story elements on paper. I think emphasizing finding the climax of the story is key; once kids can locate that, they seem to do fine with the other elements. One warning: Students will think the ending of the story is the resolution, but that is not the case. Endings represent the last event of a story while resolutions focus on *how* the conflict is solved.

We meet back on the carpet and discuss the book. Each team stands up to share and we post its work on our mountain. I like to leave this up for a while to document learning and refresh memory. After the lesson, I send them back to write a summary paragraph using the elements we just discussed. This is a great way to check for understanding.

Secret Ingredient: Use *Mufaro's Beautiful Daughters* to introduce foreshadowing.

Taking It Further

I teach the strategy of summarizing, presented in Chapter 6 of this book, throughout the year in my classroom. I weave it into almost every lesson to check for understanding. I found an excellent book by Mariann Cigrand and Phyllis Howard titled *Easy Literature-Based Quilts Around the Year* (Scholastic, 2000).

In this book, the author provides ideas and templates for making class quilts from picture books. Each student makes one quilt block out of paper and writes a summary on it, and then the blocks are posted together on a wall. I developed my own templates for the books shared in my classroom. You can see the one we created for *Mufaro's Beautiful Daughters* below. Students wrote summaries and drew the most important scenes of the story on the blocks.

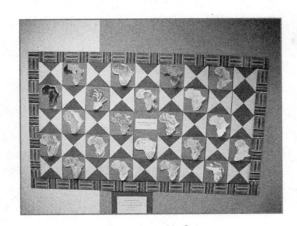

A story quilt for
Mufaro's Beautiful Daughters.

AN AFRICAN FOLK TALE

SUMMARIES OF

MUFARO'S BEAUTIFUL DAUGHTERS

BY JOHN STEPTOE

MRS. ZIMNY'S CLASS

Lesson 22:
Using the Five W's and How to Determine Importance

Rosa
Author: Nikki Giovanni
Illustrator: Bryan Collier
Scholastic, 2005

Lesson objective:
Students will use the five W's and How to determine importance in biographical text.

Rosa powerfully depicts the civil rights movement in Montgomery, Alabama. Rosa Parks, a seamstress in Montgomery, refuses to move to the back of a bus where African Americans are required to sit. Her refusal to move sets off a yearlong boycott of the buses and the eventual declaration by the U.S. Supreme Court on November 13, 1956, that segregation on buses is unconstitutional.

Students will keep their eyes trained on this book as you share it. The collages and drawings by Bryan Collier absolutely mesmerize readers. I love the expressions on the faces of the people and the quote by Martin Luther King, Jr., "We will walk until justice runs down like water and righteousness like a mighty stream." This book may be a little mature for some audiences, but any biographical picture book works well with this lesson.

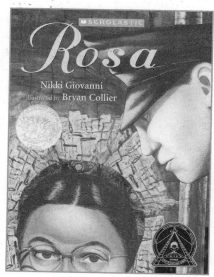

Our lesson book.

Materials

1 or more copies of *Rosa*
Large piece of butcher paper
Copies of Graphic Organizer 11: Just the Facts, page 98
News articles from a local paper
Clipboards (optional)

What to Do

1. Gather students on the reading carpet and introduce *Rosa*.

2. Read the story, allowing students to comment on the pictures and events. You will probably have to scaffold the text with some background information on the National Association for the Advancement of Colored People (NAACP) and/or explain the setting of the South in the 1950s.

3. After reading the book, pass out clipboards with Graphic Organizer 11 attached. Say to students, "You are now reporters in Montgomery, Alabama. It is November 13, 1956. A woman named Rosa Parks had caused a stir in town that has affected the community for the past year. Your job is to go out, investigate, and write an article on this event for tomorrow's paper." It is important at this point to share articles of interest from the local paper so students have an idea of what to do.

4. Say, "As I reread this story, you will pretend you are reporters. Reporters need to ask six important questions when they write news stories. This is how we make sure to get all the important information."

> WHO is involved in this story?
> WHAT happened?
> WHERE did it happen?
> WHEN did it happen?
> WHY did it happen?
> HOW did it happen?

5. Reread the story while students fill out their graphic organizers. Stop periodically so they have time to record answers to the questions.

6. After the second reading, instruct students to write the answers to the questions as a news article. (Hint: It helps when students are familiar with how newspaper articles are written, but is not necessary. You are looking to see if students are able to determine the important details in the story.)

7. Share articles and place them together on the chart paper to document the lesson.

Just the Facts

Book _____ Author _____

Who is involved in the story?
What happened?
Where did it happen?
When did it happen?
Why did it happen?
How did it happen?

Using Picture Books to Teach Comprehension Strategies

Secret Ingredient: This lesson can be repeated with other biographical picture books. It also lends itself to practicing summarizing and questioning.

Lesson 23:
Using Nonfiction Text Features to Determine Main Idea

Forest Explorer: A Life-size Field Guide
Author: Nic Bishop
Scholastic, 2004

Lesson objective:
Students will use text features in a nonfiction book to determine importance.

I found *Forest Explorer* in our school library, propped on a shelf of new titles. I was immediately drawn to the amazing, life-sized photographs that were placed into collage-like spreads. This is a beautiful nonfiction book about life in a forest. The pictures and text never fail to enthrall my students. Ladybugs, flowers, cocoons, garden snakes, nests of bunnies and birds, walking sticks, and much more fill each page with color. Nic Bishop's art makes his book a must in every classroom.

I use this book for a weeklong unit that focuses on determining importance in nonfiction text. This lesson fosters active engagement and creativity, making it one of my favorites. You can adapt any nonfiction text to support your current science or social studies units, or you can use Nic Bishop's other book, *Backyard Detective: Critters Up Close* (2002).

My students can spend hours looking at Bishop's photography.

Materials

1 or more copies of *Forest Explorer*

Large piece of chart paper

Poster paper for six teams

Markers for six teams

Highlighters for each student

4 or 5 copies of each spread in the book

The section titled "Winter Survivors" on transparency

What to Do

First Day: Gather students on the reading carpet and show them the lovely photographs in Bishop's book. I allow ample time for students to ooh and ahh over every page. They will be up on their knees and pointing to everything. Each page looks so real, you feel like you just have to touch it!

We spend several minutes on each page discussing the animals and plants and sharing stories about our own experiences in the forest. This is a terrific way to gather student background information and foster interest. Allow this first day to be for relaxing and celebrating this beautiful book. Students may want to write about their forest experiences in writing workshop.

Second Day: Discuss the table of contents and index. Bishop uses his photographs here as well, making these pages just as fascinating. You may want to spend a whole lesson teaching about how to use indexes and table of contents if you feel the need at this point.

Point out how the book is organized. The book has eight spreads that contain text. These spreads alternate with spreads of photo collages. Students might be interested to know Bishop cut and pasted more than 60 photographs to create each collage.

Rylee shares a photograph collage from *Forest Explorer*.

Choose six different text spreads for six teams of three to four students, but be sure to reserve the "Winter Survivors" section for the next day's lesson. Each group's task is to read the text for the spread it has been assigned, find the most important information, and then present that information to the rest of the class in a quick lesson. Tell students they will be the teachers for that section of the book. Because of time limits, they must teach only the important information. Pass out copies of the spreads, poster paper for presenting their information, and highlighters for locating important information in the text.

Our chart on determining importance in nonfiction texts is also helpful during science and social studies classes.

Circulate among the teams to monitor progress. At this point you are simply observing how well students can find important information. You will see many students struggling with determining importance in nonfiction; this is typical. For now, let this challenge exist. Tomorrow, students will be ready for direct instruction—they will realize their need for it.

When I first circulated among students, I immediately discovered that many of them had no idea how to find the important information. Their papers positively glowed with pink highlighter—they highlighted everything! When I asked them what the main idea of their section was, they gave me blank stares.

Third Day: On this day, have the section titled "Winter Survivors" ready on transparencies. Call students over to sit closely around you and the overhead projector. I think proximity in direct instruction is key. It sends the message that the information about to be presented is important. Model reading through "Winter Survivors" first.

Before the second reading say, "In nonfiction, an author shows main ideas by using certain methods. I will write these on the chart here to remind us of these strategies when we go back and try this again on our own sections of Nic Bishop's book." On the top of the chart write:

Some things readers can do to look for main ideas:

Look at headings and subheadings
Check out boldfaced words
Look for questions the author asks the reader
Locate topic sentences in paragraphs
Locate repeated words in the text
Look for definitions of words provided by the author
Note maps and close-ups
Listen for repeated facts

Begin to read the text again, stopping after the third paragraph and directing students to check the chart.

ME:	OK, we just read the first paragraphs. Did you notice the heading?
DANNY:	It says "Winter Survivors." It's about how creatures survive in the wintertime.
ME:	Good. What about boldfaced words?
ANGIE:	Gray squirrel, red-bellied woodpecker, and white-footed mouse. They must be important.
ME:	Well, is the whole section about these three animals?
ANGIE:	No. I think they're just examples of how to keep warm. I noticed the word warm is repeated in each paragraph.
DANNY:	I guess keeping warm is important to animals in the winter.
ME:	Good. Sounds like you've found an important detail.
JULIA:	It keeps mentioning food, too. I bet that is another important part of surviving the winter.
ME:	Excellent! I think you are right. Now we know the main idea is about surviving winter. We know finding food and keeping warm is important. The author gives us details about how different animals do this.

A student highlights important information.

After this lesson, students will return to their task with new eyes. Don't be surprised if they ask for new copies of their spreads! The old papers will be covered in pink, a reminder to kids of what happens when we think everything is important. Circulate to check for understanding. Support any student who may need one-on-one help.

Fourth Day: Allow time for students to prepare their lessons for the class. Presentations should include a summary paragraph of their assigned topic and a creative visual aid using the poster paper. Make sure they have a plan for how each student will be involved in the presentation.

Fifth Day: Watch presentations. As they present, ask students how they found the important information. Have the chart nearby and continually refer to it to scaffold learning. Post visuals, paragraphs, and the chart to document the learning.

Each team works together to determine the difference between main ideas and details.

Secret Ingredient: Use Nic Bishop's book *Backyard Detective: Critters Up Close* and this lesson plan later when focusing on summarizing.

Lesson 24:
An Assessment of Determining Importance in Fiction

The Lotus Seed
Author: Sherry Garland
Illustrator: Tatsuro Kiuchi
Scholastic, 2004

Learning objective:
To assess students' ability to determine importance in fiction.

I first became aware of *The Lotus Seed* in a few of my teacher education books. It seemed to be mentioned in every strategy instruction manual. I finally bought the book, thinking that I might as well check it out for myself. It turns out that *The Lotus Seed* works beautifully in my program. I usually share this book around Veterans Day, and once my students have read and discussed it, I ask my father to come in and talk about his experiences in Vietnam. It seems to deepen their understanding all the more.

In this story, the narrator introduces her Vietnamese grandmother, Ba. While living in Vietnam, Ba picks a lotus seed from the Imperial ponds, near the River of Perfumes. She saves the seed as a keepsake to remember and treasure the royal family. Sadly, her life is torn apart during the Vietnam War, but Ba is able to escape in a refugee boat bound for America. Arriving safely, she continues with her life, raising her children in one big house.

One day, the naughty little brother of the narrator discovers the seed and takes it. He runs out into the yard and buries it in a pool of mud, near the onion patch. Ba soon learns that her keepsake has been taken and lost. She is so devastated, she is unable to eat or sleep. True to the book's theme of renewal and hope, however, the lotus seed amazingly grows and blooms. Ba gives each of her grandchildren one of the seedpods and keeps one for herself to remember her country.

Materials

1 or more copies of *The Lotus Seed*

Double-sided copies of Graphic Organizer 12: The Most Important Word, page 105

Additional copies of *The Lotus Seed*, if possible

Clipboards

What to Do

1. Gather students to the reading area to introduce *The Lotus Seed*.

2. Say, "Today I'd like to see how well you can determine importance in fiction stories. In this activity, please don't share comments about the book or what you are writing down. This is a silent lesson because I want to know what you remember about this reading strategy."

3. Pass out clipboards with Graphic Organizer 12. The same graphic organizer should be printed on both sides.

4. Say, "Notice that your paper has the same graphic organizer on both sides. We will use the first one while we read *The Lotus Seed*. You may want to record some notes about the story. Use the front page to take notes if you like. Listen for information about character, setting, and plot. Also think about the most important word you can draw from this story."

5. Read the story without comments or discussion. Slow down at the end of each page to allow students to process information or write notes.

6. At the end of the story say, "Now you will go back to your seats and complete the second graphic organizer. In each section, write about the most important information. The boxes are small, so make sure you have only the most important details. Then write a paragraph summary of the book on notebook paper using this information. Attach the papers and turn them in to me when you are done."

7. Assess the summaries, looking for important details on characters, setting, conflict, plot, and theme. The most important word selected should be one that connects to the theme of the book.

Note: You may want to read the author's note at the back of the book before reading. This will give students valuable background information that will aid understanding. Place a world map nearby so you can point out the country of Vietnam as well.

Using Picture Books to Teach Comprehension Strategies

The Most Important Word

Book _____ Author _____

Write your most important thoughts about each story element below. Then choose one word that best connects all the story elements. Be prepared to share your word and support your choice with evidence from the story.

Characters
_____
_____
_____
_____

The Most Important Word
in this section is...

because
_____
_____

Theme
_____
_____
_____
_____

Conflict
_____
_____
_____
_____

Plot
_____
_____
_____
_____

Setting
_____
_____
_____
_____

—Presented by Valerie Bush to Central Kitsap School District and adapted from Kylene Beer's *When Kids Can't Read: What Teachers Can Do*, (2003).

Reading Workshop Link: *As students finish, ask them to draw Graphic Organizer 12 in their Reading Journals. When they are reading their books of choice during reading workshop, ask them to fill out the graphic organizer for more practice.*

Secret Ingredient: The themes of healing, forgiveness, and finding personal peace make this a valuable book in the classroom. When my father comes to my class, he tells students about the war and the landscape of Vietnam. It is fun to see my students draw comparisons to his informational talk and this fiction book, another great opportunity for comparing and contrasting. Use *The Lotus Seed* to focus on the strategy of making inferences as well.

Other Books to Teach the Strategy of Determining Importance

Bill Pickett: Rodeo-Ridin' Cowboy, by Andrea D. Pinkney

Disappearing Lake: Nature's Magic in Denali National Park, by Debbie S. Miller

There's Still Time: The Success of the Endangered Species Act, by Mark Galan

Adventures of Riley: Tigers in Teria, by Amanda Lumry and Laura Hurwitz

Wemberly Worried, by Kevin Henkes

E is for Evergreen: A Washington Alphabet, by Marie and Roland Smith

Kofi and His Magic, by Maya Angelou

Does It Always Rain in the Rain Forest?, by Melvin and Gilda Berger

Martin's Big Words, by Doreen Rappaport

Fireflies, by Julie Brinckloe

Bull Run, by Paul Fleischman

Spiders, by Gail Gibbons

Flight, by Robert Burleigh

Practice in a team environment enables students to develop the confidence they need to apply strategies on their own.

Chapter 6

Summarizing

It was early morning and my empty classroom pressed around me in unfamiliar silence. My rambunctious students had yet to invade my reflective solitude with their overstuffed backpacks and brown-bag lunches. The only sound was that of my colleague next door, singing along in her soft Southern accent with Kenny Chesney on his latest CD. I snuggled into my desk chair, hugging a cup of tea, and began to pore over ungraded projects and work yet to be done. I noticed that piles of papers had migrated from my desk to reside on the floor about my feet. Yesterday's lunch sat half eaten next to the photograph of my four children while my plan book stared up at me in its semi-empty state. Time. If only teachers had more of it.

I had to start somewhere. I reached over and grabbed yesterday's student work. As soon as I saw it, I let out a little groan. I had asked my students to write a summary of a chapter in a novel we were reading. Expecting tight paragraphs touching on the main events of the chapter, I instead found pages and pages of retellings. I saw that my students wrote about everything, including the tiniest details and the most minor characters. I knew right away that they needed some help with summarizing and it was time for me to focus on quality, not quantity.

Summarizing: A Definition

In his book *What Really Matters for Struggling Readers* (2005), Richard Allington discusses the importance of the reading strategy of summarizing. He writes,

> This is perhaps the most common and most necessary strategy. It requires that the student provide general recitation of the key content. Literate people summarize informational texts routinely in their conversations. They summarize weather reports, news articles, stock market information, and editorials. In each case, they select certain features and delete or ignore other features of the text read.

A summary captures the main ideas in a text. Unlike a retelling that includes most of the writer's message, a summary outlines main points while avoiding extraneous details and elaborations.

I think the ability to summarize is a synthesis of all the reading strategies. The reader must be able to determine importance, infer, visualize, question, and predict when developing an accurate summary. I emphasize this strategy throughout the school year, using summarizing as a way for students to articulate and condense new knowledge.

Selecting Picture Books to Support Summarizing Strategy Instruction

Here are some questions to ask as you choose books for teaching the strategy of summarizing.

◆   Does the narrative follow typical plot structures, such as rising/falling action?

◆   Do details in the story lead to one theme?

◆   Does the story emphasize a quest or problem to be solved by steps?

◆   In a nonfiction text, does the author use many details to support one main idea?

Suggestions for Teaching the Strategy of Summarizing

Valerie Bush, a literacy content facilitator for Central Kitsap School District in Washington state, has compiled suggestions for teaching summarization. She adapted the following from Fountas and Pinnell's (2001) *Guiding Readers and Writers, Grades 3-6.*

Model summary writing, beginning with short texts.

Provide examples and non-examples.

Model, share, and guide how to turn a retelling into a summary.

Have partners/whole class list characteristics of summaries and retellings.

Provide graphic organizers as scaffolds.

Allow groups to work collaboratively on summarizing.

Share group and peer summaries, elaborating on strengths and revisions as needed.

Provide sample summaries for students to evaluate and discuss.

Incorporate summarization in all content areas to review learning.

Provide opportunities for students to use summarization when sharing books.

Lesson 25:
Modeling/Scaffolding Parts of a Summary in Fictional Text

Arrowhawk
Author: Lola Schaefer
Illustrator: Gabi Swiatkowska
Henry Holt, 2004

Learning objective:
Students will use a Summary Star to understand the parts of a narrative summary.

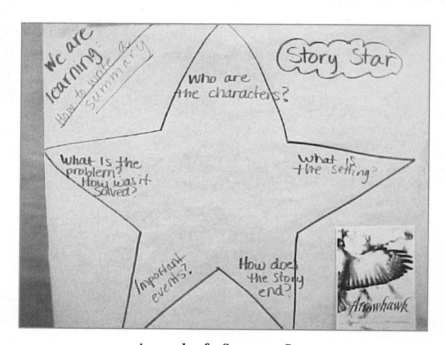

A sample of a Summary Star.

I bought *Arrowhawk* nine months before I ever used it in my classroom. I admit I was in a rush and was merely attracted to the beautiful cover and Swiatkowska's gorgeous acrylic paintings. When I had the chance to settle down and study it closely, I was a little concerned about the potentially disturbing content, because *Arrowhawk* deals with the severe injury of an animal. Later, on a rainy, restless day in my classroom that found me, once again, in a rush, I snatched it off the shelf and decided to go to the experts on this one. I would read *Arrowhawk* to my fourth graders and collect feedback on the text. I wanted to use it as an anchor book for introducing writing summaries with fictional text. To make the task more compelling, I told my students they would also have to tell me whether the book was suitable for future classes.

The story is about a red-tailed hawk that is shot with a poacher's arrow. The arrow pierces the bird's wing and leg, but amazingly does not kill it. The hawk learns to adjust to the unwanted appendage and finds a way to hunt and migrate south. One day the arrow catches on a branch and while struggling to free itself, the hawk breaks its leg.

The hawk seems to be in dire straits and near starvation when it notices a covey of sparrows. As it swoops down in an attempt to snag a meal, a net is thrown over the hawk. It ends up being tended to by the "gloved hands." The hawk has surgery, learns to eat again, and goes through a series of flying exercises until one day the leather straps that hold the hawk are cut. The bird flies away to the sound of a voice saying, "You survived, Arrowhawk. Fly home."

The real fun of this book is reading the afterword. It turns out that *Arrowhawk* is based on a true story. The hawk was spotted and tracked for eight weeks before finally being captured by raptor biologists using sparrows as bait. A fourth-grade class tracked the whereabouts of the bird by computer. The author of the book is the teacher of that class, and a preschool teacher created the illustrations.

Ben reading *Arrowhawk*.

Materials

1 or more copies of *Arrowhawk*
Copies of Graphic Organizer 13: Summary Star, page 112
Large piece of lined chart paper to model paragraph writing
Markers
Drawing paper for each team

What to Do

1. Gather students on the reading carpet and introduce *Arrowhawk*. To get my students instantly interested, I tell them I need their advice. I value their opinions, and I want to know if *Arrowhawk* is all right to use with fourth graders. I warn them that the story might be a little distressing, but that it has a happy ending.

2. I share the Summary Star graphic organizer with students. The star emphasizes the five points of a summary, providing students with a nice visual. I say, "There are five important parts to a summary. We state the main characters on one point and setting on another. We state the problem in the story on the third point and how it is resolved on the fourth, including the important events related to how the problem is solved. Finally, the ending of the story goes on the last point. We may want to include the theme or the author's message to the reader at the end of our summaries as well."

Name _____ **Graphic Organizer 13**

Summary Star

Book _____ Author _____

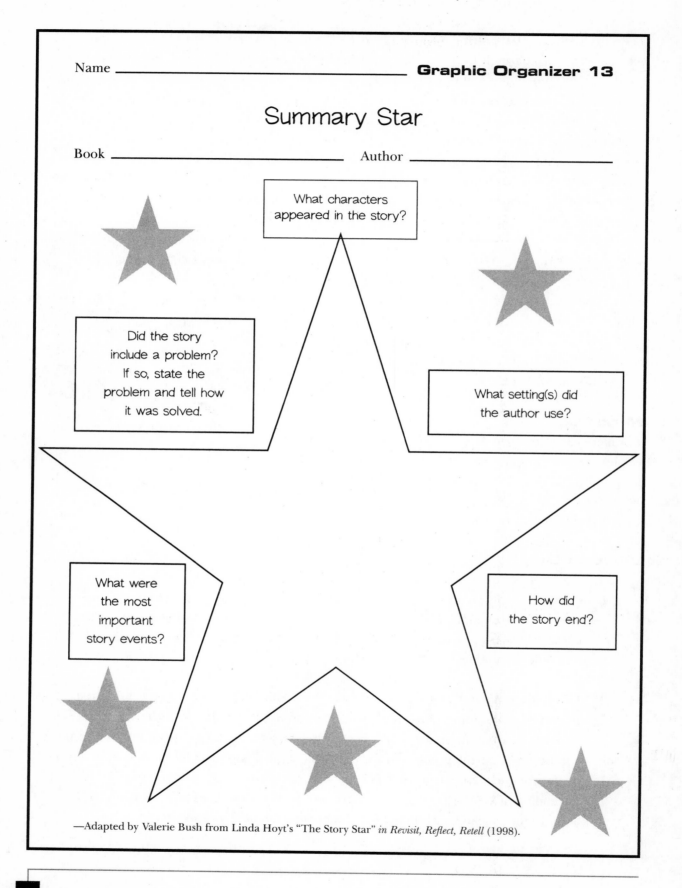

What characters
appeared in the story?

Did the story
include a problem?
If so, state the
problem and tell how
it was solved.

What setting(s) did
the author use?

What were
the most
important
story events?

How did
the story end?

—Adapted by Valerie Bush from Linda Hoyt's "The Story Star" *in Revisit, Reflect, Retell* (1998).

Using Picture Books to Teach Comprehension Strategies

3. Read the story, allowing plenty of time for discussion and comment.

4. Have groups of students fill out different points of the Summary Star. Each group is assigned to one point of the star. Groups go back to their tables and draw a picture and write a sentence for their point. Circulate among students, checking for understanding and listening to team discussions.

5. After about 15 minutes, gather again in the reading area for groups to present their part of the Summary Star and to post pictures to complete the class chart.

6. On another large piece of lined butcher paper, I work the points of the Summary Star into a summary paragraph. As I model writing it, I ask students to contribute by asking questions like, "Well, what were the important events, and how can I state them briefly?"

I write their suggestions into the paragraph, keeping it brief and concise. A good starting point is to combine setting and character into one sentence for the opening line of the paragraph. State the problem in the second line, and give the conflict and solution of the problem in the third. At the end, record the resolution of the problem and the ending. I like to add one more line that suggests why the author may have written the book for kids.

7. I present a reflection activity at the end of this lesson to get students synthesizing information in the text. I give three sentence starters:

> **I think this book should/should not be read to fourth graders because:**
> **When reading this story, I felt:**
> **The best part was:**

Students write reflections in their Reading Journals and then we gather again to share.

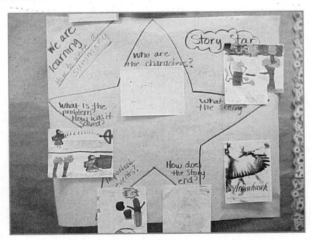

A completed summary star.

Secret Ingredient: Use *Arrowhawk* as an anchor book that reinforces making inferences. The story is told from the bird's perspective, so the book requires much inferring in order to understand it. Also, it is an excellent text for teaching how story solutions have many steps.

What Fourth Graders Said About Arrowhawk

The author did a good job drifting me into the story. There was so much description and adventure!

My favorite part was when the gloved hands held Arrowhawk.

P.S. Don't tell your class about everything. Just read the book!

I like it because it is not a boy or girl book.

This book teaches kids about lending a helping hand.

Only read it to your class next year if they deserve it and if they aren't high strung because it's kind of shocking when Arrowhawk gets shot by the poacher.

Lesson 26:
Modeling/Scaffolding Use of Story Elements When Summarizing Fictional Text

Frog Girl
Author and Illustrator: Paul Owen Lewis
Tricycle Press, 1997

Learning objective:
Students will use story elements to write a summary of fictional text.

Frog Girl, a story about a Northwest coastal tribe, became a personal favorite of mine because the setting takes place right where I live. If you have not studied the artwork or story patterns of the indigenous people of Washington state or coastal Canada, this book is a terrific introduction. I also discovered that the author, Paul Owen Lewis, lived just a ferry ride away from my classroom. I invited him in and he shared his beautiful work with my students.

In the story, a coastal chieftain's daughter witnesses two naughty boys capturing frogs. When the boys run off, a small frog left over from the amphibious kidnapping, pleads for the girl to follow it. It lifts up the lake and jumps below. The girl follows. There, she comes to an underwater village, inhabited by strange frog people. She listens to the elderly grandmother grieve for her captured children. The intensity of the grandmother's misery is transported into the campfire, which begins to erupt violently like a volcano.

The girl is magically transported back to the shore of the lake. She hurries to her own village and finds it threatened by an erupting volcano in the distance. She searches the evacuated village until she finds the basket of trapped frogs. She runs with them to the lakeside and sets them free, appeasing the volcano before it can destroy her village.

Because *Frog Girl* follows a basic story structure, I like to use the elements of character, setting, conflict, important events, solution, and theme to help students construct a strong narrative summary. I have adapted this idea from Valerie Bush, my district Literacy Content Facilitator.

Materials

1 or more copies of *Frog Girl*

Copies of Graphic Organizer 14: Element Pyramid, page 117

Large piece of chart paper with the graphic organizer drawn on it

Markers

Sticky notes for each student

What to Do

1. Call students to the reading area and introduce *Frog Girl*. Discuss the artwork of coastal Northwest tribes.

2. Draw attention to the chart paper posted on the wall nearby. Say, "This is what I call an Element Pyramid. It will help us to look at story elements to write summaries. Do you see the base of the pyramid? It is one big block. When we finish the story, this is where we write our personal response to *Frog Girl*. Next, we have three blocks: one for the character, one for setting, and one for the problem. In the middle of the pyramid we have two blocks. In one block we will write the steps to solve the problem. The second box will contain the resolution. At the top of the pyramid, we have just one block. Here we will record the author's purpose or theme of the story. In other words, we'll determine why Paul Owen Lewis wrote this book for kids."

3. Read the story. Have students help fill out the Element Pyramid during the reading, or you can simply let them enjoy the story first and work on the chart paper when you are finished reading. Allow for ample discussion and response to the story. It is quite unusual because it contains many Northwest coastal motifs. Be prepared for some great discussions.

Northwest Coastal Tribal Story Motifs
(Adapted from Paul Owen Lewis's Author Notes in *Storm Boy*.)

Separation: Wandering too far from the safety of the village
                    Mysterious entrances into the spirit world

Initiation: Animals take on human form
                    Experience of potlatching, or exchange of gifts and traditions

Return: Symbolic object given to assist return to reality
                    Restoration to community by continual wishing
                    Distortion of time
                    Claiming of a tribal crest

Element Pyramid

Book _____ Author _____

Theme

Problem-Solving Steps	Solution

Character(s)	Setting	Problem/Conflict

My Personal Response:

4. Start completing the Element Pyramid by recording the main characters, setting, and the problem or conflict in the story.

5. Discuss and fill out the two problem-solving boxes. I make sure to go back and reread parts of the story to make this clearer. Readers often neglect these steps when they become engrossed in a story. Record the resolution as well.

6. Together, discuss why Paul Owen Lewis wrote the book for kids and record the reason under Theme.

Name _____ **Graphic Organizer 14**

Element Pyramid

Book _____ Author _____

Theme

Children should be kind and compassionate toward Mother Nature's creatures.

Problem-Solving Steps

A frog tells Frog Girl her relatives have been stolen by some local boys. Frog Girl travels under the lake to meet Grandmother, who grieves for her lost children. Frog Girl travels back to her village to discover the captured frogs.

Solution

Frog Girl releases the captured frogs back into the lake, avoiding a volcanic catastrophe.

Character(s)

Frog Girl, frog friend, Grandmother of the frogs, two village boys

Setting

A coastal village near a volcano and lake

Problem/Conflict

Two village boys steal frogs from the lake, upsetting nature and triggering a volcanic disruption that endangers the village.

My Personal Response:

We enjoyed learning about the way coastal Native Americans told stories to their children. Our favorite page was when Frog Girl ran with the basket of frogs and the volcano was erupting behind her. Our favorite character was Grandmother because her hat looked like a smoking volcano.

Using Picture Books to Teach Comprehension Strategies

7. I like to save the Personal Response section at the base for the very last. At this point, students have discussed the story at length. Students can now record their personal responses to *Frog Girl* on a sticky note. Students come up to share their responses and place them in the Personal Response section on the chart.

8. For teams or individual practice, ask students to take the information from the Element Pyramid to write a paragraph summary. Collect the paragraphs to assess progress or have students share them with the group. If students are still challenged by writing summary paragraphs, use lined chart paper to model putting the information into a summary.

Sentence Starters for Personal Response

My favorite character was . . . because . . .
My favorite scene was . . . because . . .
The author did a good job at . . .
This story made me feel . . .
One lesson I learned from this story is . . .
This book reminds me of . . .
I am like the main character because . . .
I am not like the main character because . . .
I thought the setting was . . . because . . .
I wish the author would have . . .
I would share this book with future classes because . . .
I wouldn't share this book because . . .
I am wondering . . .

Reading Workshop Link: *As students read on their own, ask them to draw an Element Pyramid in their Reading Journals or provide them with a copy of Graphic Organizer 16. After students fill out the Element Pyramid during silent reading, use the last few minutes of reading workshop to write summaries of what was read and then have them share.*

Lesson 27:
Scaffolding Use of Summarizing to Develop a Compare/Contrast Paragraph

Storm Boy
Author and Illustrator: Paul Owen Lewis
Tricycle Press, 1999

Learning objective:
Students will summarize two stories and compare the story elements in them.

Paul Owen Lewis's book *Storm Boy* is the perfect story to follow *Frog Girl* because the plots and Native American motifs are quite similar. In this tale, a coastal chieftain's son falls into the sea during a storm and sinks to the bottom, where he encounters a strange underwater village. The people are enormous, resembling orcas. The orca people invite the boy into a mysterious lodge, where he learns new dances and devours raw fish. After a time, he travels on the fin of one of the orcas until he reaches the surface. He swims back to his home village, where his mother tells him he has been lost for an entire year.

Frog Girl and *Storm Boy* are comparable because they follow the traditional format of native tales. Northwest coast story motifs include a period of separation from family and then a mysterious entrance into a spirit world, where animals become human-like and inanimate objects have emotions, like the angry volcano in *Frog Girl*. A period of potlatching with other beings follows. During this time, there may be an exchange of gifts, stories, dances, and other traditions. Finally, the visitor develops an intense wish to return to the family village, and eventually he or she does.

Lewis carefully provides these elements in both books, making them easy to compare and contrast. You may want to use this lesson as an assessment or simply for further practice.

Materials
Copies of *Storm Boy* and *Frog Girl*
Large piece of chart paper
Markers

What to Do

1. Gather students on the reading carpet and introduce *Storm Boy*. Keep a copy of *Frog Girl* nearby. Share the pictures and remind students that Paul Owen Lewis wrote both books.

2. Compare the illustrations in both books by asking two students to hold the books open. Compare the native coastal art and the illustrations of villages. Stress what is common in both books.

3. Say, "You are quickly becoming experts in summarizing stories. Today I think we are ready to try an advanced activity. Let's compare *Storm Boy* and *Frog Girl*. We will have to use some summarizing in order to do this."

4. On the chart paper draw five Venn diagrams. Say, "Remember when we used elements of a story to summarize? Can you tell me the elements once again and I will record them next to the Venn diagrams?" As students volunteer them, write the name of each element next to a different diagram.

5. Read *Storm Boy*, asking students simply to listen. You might suggest that they think about *Frog Girl* as you read it so they can compare the two stories later. Allow comments on the artwork and plot as you proceed.

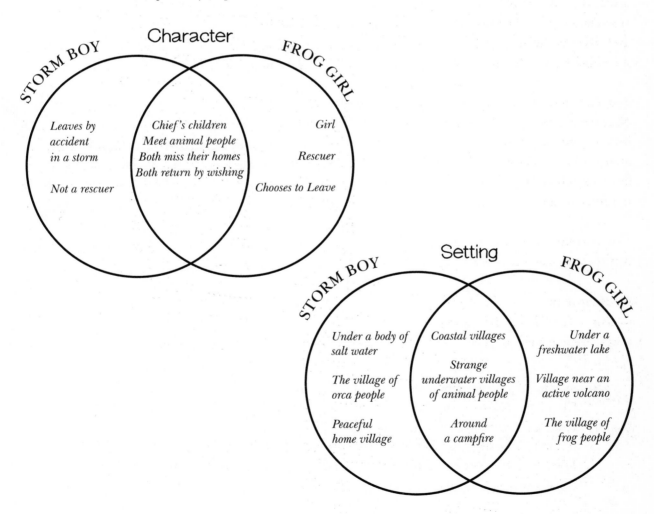

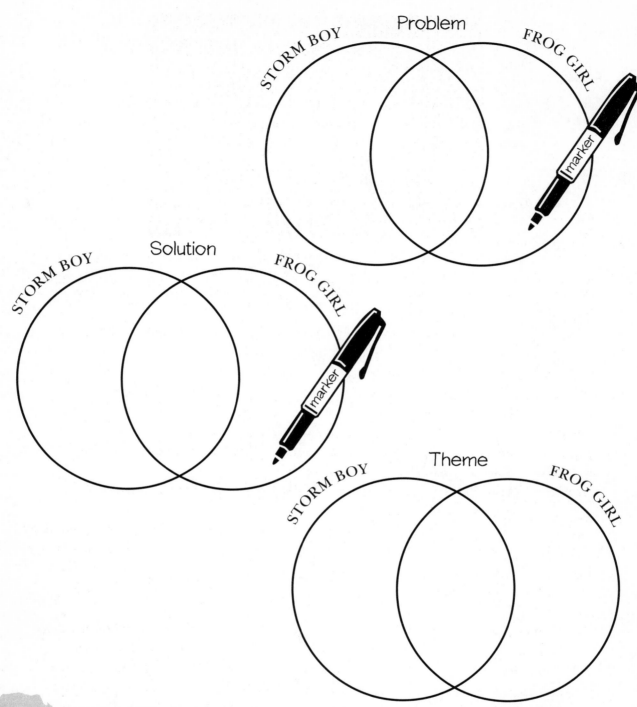

Problem

STORM BOY   FROG GIRL

Solution

STORM BOY   FROG GIRL

Theme

STORM BOY   FROG GIRL

6. When you finish the book, turn to the Venn diagram on the chart paper that is labeled Character. Ask students to compare the two main characters of each story. Say, "In the circle labeled Frog Girl, let's write what we know about the main character. In the circle labeled Storm Boy, we will write what we know about the boy in that story. We will record ideas about how the two characters are the same where the two circles overlap. Differences will be recorded on the circles, but not where they overlap."

Using Picture Books to Teach Comprehension Strategies

Ben, Julia, and Adam reading outdoors.

ME:	Think about both of the main characters. How are they different or alike?
JAMES:	One's a boy and one's a girl.
ME:	OK. Those are definitely differences. [I record "girl" and "boy" in the corresponding circles for *Storm Boy* and *Frog Girl*.]
ALLISON:	Frog Girl is a hero. I don't think Storm Boy is. He's just lost.
ME:	That's very true. She has to save her village. Storm Boy's village is safe. [Record on the chart for differences.]
GABBI:	Yeah, he's lost, but Frog Girl chooses to leave her village.
ME:	So Storm Boy gets lost in a storm, but Frog Girl leaves by her own choice. She wants to rescue the village.
TONY:	Yeah, but they both meet strange animal people and become friends. That would be the same.
ME:	That is an important similarity. [I record this on the overlapping area of the circles.]
GABBI:	Their dads are both chiefs. That makes them the same, too. It means their families are important.
ME:	Excellent. [I record this as well.]

7. Continue to fill out the other diagrams. Ask students to write five paragraphs using the information on the chart. In each paragraph, they are to summarize both stories by comparing the elements of character, setting, problem, resolution, and theme. You can also use this as an assessment or as an extension for students who need more of a challenge. Remember, this is a more complex activity because several skills are needed. Students must be able to recall and understand the elements of story, compare and contrast two stories, and summarize in writing. Use this lesson when students have become quite proficient at summarization.

Secret Ingredient: Use Paul Owen Lewis's books to explore Native American art. The Internet offers numerous crest patterns that can be copied and applied in art lessons.

Lesson 28:
Using the Summary Frame to Accurately Summarize

Little Oh
Author: Laura Krauss Melmed
Illustrator: Jim LaMarche
HarperCollins, 1997

Learning objective:
Students will use a Summary Frame to write an accurate summary of a narrative.

I love *Little Oh* because it is suffused with human emotion, particularly loneliness. From the descriptive words of Laura Krauss Melmed to the captivating illustrations of Jim LaMarche, students will be entranced by the array of feelings portrayed in this Japanese fantasy story. From loneliness to wonderment to fear to exhaustion to peace, this book has it all. The story follows a perfect plot format of rising/falling action. This flexible lesson can be used to introduce, scaffold, or assess students. Literacy Content Facilitator Valerie Bush adapted the idea for this lesson from Maureen Aumann's *Step Up to Writing* (2003).

In this beautiful tale, a lonely woman makes an origami girl reminiscent of a little pink valentine. The woman puts her in a box and awakens the next morning to find that the little paper doll has come to life. It cries, "Good morning, Mother!" The precocious doll names herself "Little Oh" after her mother's amazed response.

The woman and the origami girl become close and the woman feels less lonely. Little Oh, however, hears children playing outside. She wants to run and play too, but Mother says it is much too dangerous. One day, the mother packs her little paper daughter into a basket and they travel to town. A dog upturns the basket and the doll falls out, narrowly escaping the hound. She has many adventures, including floating down a river and getting picked up by a heron, which offers to fly her home.

Unfortunately, the heron mistakenly leaves Little Oh at the wrong house. She peeks into the window and spies a man with his son. She knows this is not Mother's house and she miserably huddles down into a flowerpot. Eventually, the man and boy find Little Oh and notice she has an address written on her back. They realize it is the home right next door, so they return the origami girl to the lonely woman. When the hands of the man and woman touch, the paper doll turns into a human girl and they all become a complete family.

Materials

1 or more copies of *Little Oh*

Chart paper

Markers

Lined paper

Clipboards

What to Do

A student's summary frame.

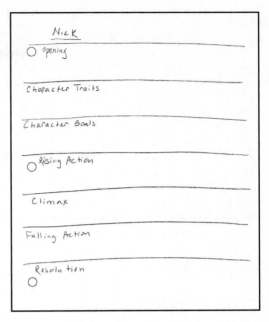

1. Gather students on the carpet and introduce *Little Oh*. It is a good idea to read this book the day before, just to let students enjoy it. The next day, read the story again to work on the summarization strategy.

2. Say, "We have been working on the summarizing strategy in our reading. I would like to see how you are doing with this strategy. Today, you will work on your own to write a summary of *Little Oh*."

3. Say, "On your paper, draw seven sections on the front. Save the back of the paper for your summary."

4. Ask students to label each section as follows:

   1. Opening (story start)
   2. Character traits (names/descriptions)
   3. Character goals (what the main character is trying to accomplish)
   4. Rising action (events leading to the problem or conflict)
   5. Climax (problem/conflict effect on the character)
   6. Falling action (immediate aftermath of climax)
   7. Resolution (final results of the solved problem)

5. As you read, ask students to fill out each section with only one sentence. They may use two sentences if they just can't work it into one. Sentences should look like the following:
   1. A lonely woman sits in her house and creates an origami girl.
   2. The paper doll comes alive, surprising the lonely woman. The doll names herself Little Oh.
   3. The lonely woman wants a daughter, and Little Oh wants to be a real child so she can play outside.

4. One day when they go to town, the woman accidentally drops Little Oh in the street and loses her, setting off a series of adventures.

5. A heron mercifully takes Little Oh home, but leaves her at the wrong house. Little Oh huddles in a flowerpot and becomes hopelessly lonely for her human mother, wishing for the security and love of home.

6. A man and his son discover Little Oh on their porch with an address written on her back.

7. When they return Little Oh to the lonely woman's house, the hands of the man and woman touch, turning Little Oh into a real child and the entire group into a new family.

6. Ask students to return to their seats to write a summary of *Little Oh* on the back of their papers. Remind them to refer to the seven boxes for help.

7. Assess papers and ask students to practice using the seven steps during reading workshop, recording the information in their Reading Journals.

Secret Ingredient: Extend this lesson into writing workshop, where students construct personal narratives. Use the seven steps pattern to outline stories in a prewriting activity.

Lesson 29:
Writing a Brief Summary of Fictional Text

Lon Po Po: A Red-Riding Hood Story From China
Author and Illustrator: Ed Young
Philomel Books, 1989

Learning objective:
Students will use a word pyramid to practice brevity in summarization.

I don't think any child should go through elementary school without experiencing *Lon Po Po*, a Chinese rendition of Little Red Riding Hood. Young's illustrations are so positively haunting that he was awarded the 1990 Caldecott Medal. When I read the dedication page, I was immediately drawn in:

> *To all the wolves in the world*
> *For lending their good name*
> *As a tangible symbol*
> *For our darkness.*

The story opens with a woman living in her country home with her three children, named Shang, Tao, and Paotze. On Grandmother's birthday, Mother leaves the children to go pay homage. She warns the children to bolt the door tight at sunset.

Of course, Wolf shows up at night pretending to be Po Po, or "grandmother." Wolf enters the house and crawls into bed with the children. In the dark, the children go through the questioning ritual by asking the disguised wolf why his voice is so low. Shang, the eldest and cleverest, finally lights a candle to see what's going on, but Wolf blows it out. Fortunately, she quickly glimpses the intruder and devises a plan to kill the wolf.

She tempts the wolf outside for the gingko nuts growing in a large tree. Wolf tells the children to climb up and get the nuts for him. Shang tells "Po Po" to get a basket and a rope so they can pull him up, too. The children pull up the wolf, and as he nears the top, they release the rope and Wolf falls to his death.

This is another tale that would be perfect for the Summary Star Graphic Organizer (page 112) or a compare/contrast with the European version of Little Red Riding Hood. Don't assume children know the tale. I am increasingly finding that my students have little familiarity with classic fairy tales. This saddens me because fairy tales are such a wonderful foundation for understanding story meaning, culture, and symbolism. The following lesson was adapted by Valerie Bush.

Materials

1 or more copies of *Lon Po Po*

Copies of Graphic Organizer 15: Summary Game, page 129

Chart paper

Markers

What to Do

1. Call students to the reading carpet and introduce *Lon Po Po*. I like to show the pictures first and listen to students' comments about Ed Young's amazing artwork. One student pointed out that the terrain on the first page, when mother waves good-bye, is actually the snout of a wolf. In all my years I have of reading *Lon Po Po*, I had never noticed this.

2. Say, "Today we will play a summarizing game. This game will help us to be brief when we summarize a story." Draw the Summary Game on the chart paper and pass out the graphic organizer to each student. Say, "While I read the book, think about ways to fill out the sheet to briefly summarize *Lon Po Po*. For now, let's just enjoy the story. When I read it a second time, you can begin to fill out your graphic organizer."

3. Read *Lon Po Po*. Allow for discussion and comments from students as you explore each page. Discuss the illustrations and what makes them so frightening. Talk about the characters and their motives and evaluate the author's ability to develop the mood. Keep the discussion open. The main goal is to get students thinking about the book.

4. After the first reading, ask students to pick up their graphic organizers. Give them a few minutes to look them over. Many students will begin to fill them out. Say, "As I read *Lon Po Po* a second time, see if you can play the game by filling out the graphic organizer. At the end, we will combine our answers and fill out the chart paper."

5. Read the story again, this time asking students to remain quiet as they write and think.

6. At the end of the second reading, have students volunteer to fill out the lines on the chart.

7. After filling out the class graphic organizer on the chart paper, students can take the Summary Game and put the words into a summary paragraph. They can also draw Summary Games in their Reading Journals and use this activity while they read in reading workshop.

Secret Ingredient: Use *Lon Po Po* when teaching the prediction strategy.

Summary Game: Limit Your Words

Book _____ Author _____

_____

Name of main character

_____   _____

2 words to describe the character

_____   _____   _____

3 words to describe the setting

_____   _____   _____   _____

4 words to state the conflict in the story

_____   _____   _____   _____   _____

5 words to describe the first main event

_____   _____   _____   _____   _____   _____

6 words to describe the second main event

_____   _____   _____   _____   _____   _____   _____

7 words to describe the third main event

_____   _____   _____   _____   _____   _____   _____   _____

8 words to state the resolution

Summary Game: Limit Your Words

Book _____ Author _____

Shang
_____
Name of main character

Clever   Eldest
_____   _____
2 words to describe the character

Isolated   Chinese   Home
_____   _____   _____
3 words to describe the setting

Wolf   might   eat   Shang
_____   _____   ___   _____
4 words to state the conflict in the story

Shang   climbs   the   gingko   tree
_____   _____   ___   _____   ____
5 words to describe the first main event

Shang   offers   to   pull   Wolf   up
_____   _____   __   ____   ____   __
6 words to describe the second main event

Shang   drops   Wolf   as   he   nears   top
_____   _____   ____   __   __   _____   ___
7 words to describe the third main event

Wolf's   heart   breaks   into   pieces   when   he   falls
_____   _____   _____   ____   _____   ____   __   _____
8 words to state the resolution

Lesson 30:
Summarizing Nonfiction

Getting to Know the World's Greatest Artists Series
Author and Illustrator: Mike Venezia
Children's Press, 1988

"What happened?" shouts Robbie as he stands in the doorway of our classroom early Monday morning. Fellow students push in behind him, eager to see what is going on. I watch their mouths open and backpacks drop to the floor in surprise.

"Where are we supposed to sit?" they ask as they tentatively enter the room.

"Well," I say, "this week is going to be slightly different, so put your backpacks away and come sit with me on the floor."

My students at the beginning of our art unit.

My wary students move into the room where they find desks and tables pushed against the walls. Every poster has been removed from two walls and in the center of the room, a large blue tarp covers the carpet. The tarp is covered with art supplies such as poster board, coffee cans of paintbrushes, bottles of paint, yardsticks, pencils, paper cups, plates, and paper towels. The best part, however, is the stack of art books from library. I invite students to sit with me around the tarp and we begin one of my favorite lessons.

Why is it my favorite? During the winter doldrums or end-of-the-year transition to summer break, I love surprising my students with this weeklong study of Mike Venezia's Getting to Know the World's Greatest Artists picture books. The room, no longer a fourth-grade classroom, becomes a wonderful art studio. We read books from the series on individual artists such as Vincent Van Gogh, Leonardo da Vinci, Claude Monet, Georgia O'Keeffe, Salvador Dali, Pablo Picasso, and many more. These little paperbacks are as affordable as a magazine and worth every cent.

Don't let the simple text in Venezia's books fool you. There is a lot going on. He covers the artist's biographical information, major works, and the development of his or her style and medium. In *Picasso*, for instance, Venezia explains the development of cubism and abstract art in a clear student- and teacher-friendly way.

Materials

For each student: White poster board
Yardstick
Paint
Photocopy of a masterpiece by a great artist
Paint
Brushes
White note cards
Copies of Graphic Organizer 16: Frayer Model
for Nonfiction, page 133

One of our lesson books.

What to Do

1. Gather students around the tarp and introduce Venezia's books. Say, "You have become experts at summarizing stories. Let's see what we can do with some information from a nonfiction book. I'd like you to study a famous artist of your choice and write a summary about your artist to share with the class. You will read a lot of information, so you will have to decide what is important and what isn't. Remember, this is just a summary, not a research report."

2. Share Venezia's books with students and discuss. It's fun to see which artistic styles students appreciate the most. Use the time to share and discuss style differences.

3. Hand out Graphic Organizer 16: Frayer Model for Nonfiction. Ask students to write the name of their artist in the center box. They will read about their artist, looking specifically for background, famous works (examples), and essential characteristics of the works, such as color, medium, and style. Finally, students are to provide non-examples. Non-examples would be the work of other artists during the same time period. Students will write a summary of this information onto a note card.

4. Students select a major work by their artist. Photocopy the picture of the masterpiece. Black-and-white copies are fine. Students should refer to the masterpiece in the book for color information.

Cameron watches as his team begins to duplicate a Van Gogh painting.

Using Picture Books to Teach Comprehension Strategies

Frayer Model for Nonfiction

Book _____ Author _____

Background of the Artist	Examples (Famous works)

Essential Characteristics of Works

Non-Examples
(Other artists and works during his/her time)

—Adapted from Marzano, Pickering, and Pollack's *Classroom Instruction That Works* (2001).

5. Using a ruler and pencil, students draw a grid right on their photocopies in 1-inch squares. Then, students transfer the grid onto the large poster board, but on a larger scale. I usually use 1 inch = 4 inches, but this will vary with each painting.

6. Students copy onto the poster board, grid by grid. This process keeps the paintings to scale and enables students to draw them much more accurately than if they were drawn freehand.

7. Be patient. This project takes several days, so sit back and enjoy it. You will see your students become engrossed in art. When we created our museum, beautiful paintings lined the wall and students had a real sense of accomplishment. Place students' notecards (see Step 3) under their paintings.

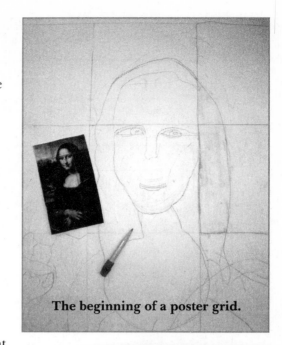

The beginning of a poster grid.

A Georgia O'Keefe project in process.

Other Books to Teach the Summarizing Strategy

Ride Like the Wind: A Tale of the Pony Express, by Bernie Fuchs

The Toughest Cowboy, by John Frank

The Village of Round and Square Houses, by Ann Grifalconi

The Legend of the Bluebonnet, by Tomie DePaola

Hog Music, by M. C. Helldorfer

The Paint Box, by Maxine Trottier

John Muir: America's Naturalist, by Thomas Locker and M. D. Edgar

Kat Kong, by Dav Pilkey

Charlie Anderson, by Barbara Abercrombie

The Wednesday Surprise, by Eve Bunting

Appendix

Learning Objective:

While studying several books by the same author, students will practice comparing and contrasting stories and making inferences.

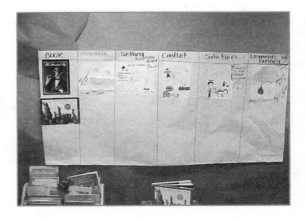

Our chart for a Chris Van Allsburg author study.

I love to use Chris Van Allsburg's surreal picture books as an author study. The author study allows me to reinforce the strategy of making inferences and to introduce narrative story elements. During the unit, students also practice comparing and contrasting, evaluating, and summarizing. I spend three weeks on this unit, and I like to begin with *The Sweetest Fig* because it is usually a less familiar title for students. *The Sweetest Fig* is a bizarre story of a cruel Parisian dentist named Bibot. The story opens with Bibot approaching his dog Marcel (played once again by the bull terrier Fritz) with a rolled newspaper in hand. Bibot plans on punishing little Marcel for sitting on his furniture. Then the book cuts away to Bibot at his office, where a mysterious elderly woman asks him for help. Her tooth is causing her terrible pain. Bibot fixes the tooth, but without any pain medication, and then asks for payment. The woman tries to pay with two figs, which she promises will make his dreams come true. Bibot, in a rage, sends her away without any pills to ease the pain.

That night, he eats a fig, falls asleep, and wakes the next morning to find that, indeed, his dream has come true—he is walking through the streets of Paris in his underwear! He returns home and spends many days training his mind to dream he is the richest man in the world. Finally, he decides to eat the second fig, but tricky Marcel gets there first. He gobbles up the sweetest fig, only to dream that night that he is the master and Bibot is the dog.

Some of our author study books on display.

Materials

Copies of the books listed on page 135 (as many copies as possible)

Large chart paper with six columns. Starting from the left, title each column:

      Book (hang a photocopy of *The Sweetest Fig* book cover here)

      Characters

      Setting

      Conflict

      Solution

      Elements of Fantasy

Blue marker

Paper and markers for groups

What to Do

1. After sharing and enjoying *The Sweetest Fig* together, assign groups of three to five students one of the items listed on the chart (characters, setting (including mood), conflict, solution, and elements of fantasy). Tell students they are to depict the item in a picture as well as in a written paragraph.

2. If you have read *The Widow's Broom* already, students will usually begin by comparing this book with it. For example, some of my students noticed that the elderly woman in *The Sweetest Fig* looks exactly like Minna Shaw in *The Widow's Broom*. They commented on Fritz's recurrence in almost all of Van Allsburg's books, and the author's creation of illustrations by using tiny dots. We talked about the lack of color, the rounded and angular shapes of objects in the stories (Van Allsburg was a sculptor),

Students comparing Van Allsburg's books.

and the recurrence of certain words and themes. The elements of fantasy team noticed that there were three magical events in *The Sweetest Fig*, and compared this to the use of the number three in *The Widow's Broom*. I always review the elements of fantasy at this point. Writing the elements on a chart and posting them in the classroom helps too. (See page 37 for the elements of fantasy list.)

3. Have teams return to the reading carpet. Invite each team to come up, read its collaborative paragraph, explain the drawing, answer class questions, and post the work on the butcher paper chart on the first row.

   Note: This lesson will still work well if you and your students have not read *The Widow's Broom*. Students can just describe the elements in *The Sweetest Fig*.

4. After some discussion, I send my students back to their seats to write paragraph summaries of the book individually. The paragraphs should state the characters, setting, problem, and solution.

5. Next, I move on to *The Garden of Abdul Gasazi* and read it with my students. The interplay of light and shadow in this book makes it visually stunning. Miss Hester, owner of a somewhat passive-aggressive and mischievous dog named Fritz, asks her neighbor, a boy named Alan, to dog-sit. While watching Fritz, Alan strives valiantly to keep the little terrier out of trouble. When they go

for a walk, Fritz gets away from Alan and scampers into a garden owned by a retired magician named Abdul Gasazi. The garden is completely forbidden to dogs. Alan searches through the garden and ends up meeting Gasazi, who informs Alan that Fritz has been turned into a duck as a punishment for trespassing. By the way, punishment of terriers in almost all of Van Allsburg's books is always delightfully noted by students. The duck snatches Alan's hat and flies away. Alan returns to Miss Hester's to tell her about her pet's sad demise. Miss Hester chastises Alan for believing such nonsense and shows him that Fritz had long since returned home, in the form of a dog. Embarrassed, Alan departs. But Van Allsburg almost always gives a little twist at the end of his books. Outside Alan discovers the naughty Fritz holding Alan's hat in his mouth. This ending leaves lots of room for making inferences!

6. Repeat the activity previously done with *The Sweetest Fig*, but assign a new element to each group. For example, the team that worked on character in the last lesson might work on setting.

After 15 minutes of work time, meet on the carpet to have each team share. As students share, they will begin comparing the two books. Listen for comparisons that lead to greater understanding of text, including interpretation through inferring.

JASON: Mrs. Zimny, in *The Sweetest Fig*, Fritz plays a good guy. In *The Garden of Abdul Gasazi*, he's really bad.

MAGGIE: Yeah, and I notice that there is a magic person in each story. The old woman in *The Sweetest Fig* and then the magician.

GABBI: But we don't really know if the magician is magic. Maybe nothing really happened and he was just teasing.

JASON: Then how did Fritz get the hat? If the magician was just teasing, he's mean and he hates dogs.

ANDREW: And if the magician was just joking around, the book isn't a fantasy book at all. It would just be realistic fiction. Does Van Allsburg write realistic fiction?

7. After teams share, we tape their work on the chart in *The Sweetest Fig* section. As students discuss, I use a blue marker to record their comparisons directly on the chart between the two books. See the picture at the right.

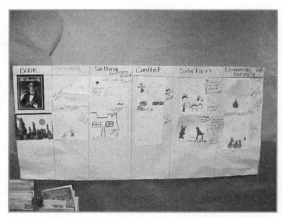

Our comparison chart in process.

Using Picture Books to Teach Comprehension Strategies

8. For individual practice, students can write a summarizing paragraph in their reading journals.

9. Next, I share *Two Bad Ants*. This book is somewhat different from Van Allsburg's other books. Students notice Van Allsburg uses lines to create his illustrations rather than dots or points as he did in his other books. Also, there seems to be nothing magical in this book. In *Two Bad Ants*, an ant returns to the nest with a white jewel that pleases the queen. She devours this bit of sugar and begs for more.

A close-up of our chart.

Off the ants go, trailing through a deep forest of grass, up a mountain-like wall, and into a kitchen. When the last two ants in line discover the sugar bowl, they decide it is so wonderful they cannot possibly leave. This turns out to be a bad decision, as they end up in all kinds of frightening situations. They fall into a cup of coffee, get roasted in the toaster, and almost drown in a faucet waterfall. Fortunately, they come to their senses and return to their safe nest with the others. Encourage students to have fun discovering how very different *Two Bad Ants* is from Van Allsburg's other stories.

Some of my students noticed the following:
It has more color.
There are no antagonists.
The pictures are created with line.
There is a straightforward, happy ending.
There is no Fritz!
There are no magical occurrences.

10. Repeat the same steps and activities as you did for *The Sweetest Fig* and *The Garden of Abdul Gasazi*. Continue to write comparisons that students note on the chart with the blue marker, modeling thinking strategies.

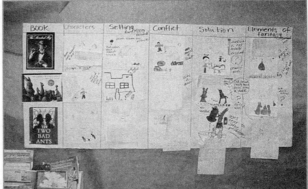
Our completed chart.

Final Assessment: This assessment will have your classroom humming quietly like a beehive. It tests two things: the ability to compare/contrast text and the ability to use inferring strategies to increase understanding.

At the conclusion of the Van Allsburg author study, I read *Jumanji* to my students. This is an action-packed story in which two somewhat irresponsible children find a magical game in a park. They are ominously warned to finish the game if they choose to play it. (By the way, most Van Allsburg stories include a warning to a somewhat naughty person or animal.) As in a lot of books by Van Allsburg, the children fail to heed the warning and trouble begins. The jungle game brings a real lion, a troop of monkeys, an erupting volcano, and a stampede of rhinos into their home. Fortunately, the game ends just in time and the children are saved.

Before I share this story, I tell students that this lesson is an assessment. So, unlike other times when we read, they will not be allowed to discuss or comment. When they are done hearing the story, they are to compare and contrast *Jumanji* with one of the other Chris Van Allsburg books we have read. Students are to find three similarities and three differences and write about them.

My students have always taken this assessment very seriously. They go back to their seats and begin writing. The Van Allsburg books are silently passed around so students can refer to them for more information. I always find this assessment activity very rewarding. All the modeling, active engagement, and discussion the author study has provided results in students confidently and successfully completing the task.

Secret Ingredient: During writing workshop, share the pictures in the Van Allsburg book *The Mysteries of Harris Burdick*. Ask students to choose a picture and write a creative story for it. They will have to infer what is happening in the picture in order to write. Poster-size copies of the illustrations are also available through book dealers. Make a display with the posters and post stories near them.

Bibliography ·········· Children's Books Cited

Abercrombie, B. (1995). *Charlie Anderson*. New York: Aladdin.

Anderson, H. C., & Pinkney, J. (1999). *The little match girl*. New York: Puffin.

Angelou, M., & Courtney-Clark, M. (1996). *Kofi and his magic*. New York: Clarkson N. Potter.

Berger, M., & Berger, G. (2001). *Does it always rain in the rain forest?* New York: Scholastic.

Bishop, N. (2004). *Forest explorer: A life-size field guide*. New York: Scholastic.

Bishop, N. (2002). *Backyard detective: Critters up close*. New York: Scholastic.

Blomgren, J. (2004). *Where would I be in an evergreen tree?* Seattle, WA: Sasquatch.

Brett, J. (2002). *Who's that knocking on Christmas Eve?* New York: Putnam.

Brinckloe, J. (1985). *Fireflies*. New York: Simon & Schuster.

Bruchac, J., & Locker, J. (1992). *Thirteen moons on Turtle's back*. New York: Philomel.

Bunting, E. (2001). *Dandelions*. New York: Harcourt.

Bunting, E. (2001) *Gleam and glow*. New York: Harcourt.

Bunting, E. (2000). *The memory string*. New York: Clarion

Bunting, E. (1996). *Train to Somewhere*. New York: Clarion.

Bunting, E. (1992). *The wall*. New York: Clarion.

Bunting, E. (1990). *How many days to America?* New York: Clarion

Bunting, E., & Carrick, D. (1989). *The Wednesday surprise*. New York: Clarion.

Burleigh, R. (1997). *Flight*. New York: Putnam.

Buzzeo, T. (2002). *The sea chest*. New York: Dial.

DePaola, T. (1983). *The legend of the bluebonnet*. New York: Putnam.

Donovan, J. (2004). *Winter's gift*. Chelsea, MI: Sleeping Bear Press.

Dorros, A. (1997). *Abuela*. New York: Puffin.

Dwyer, M. (1997). *Aurora: A tale of the northern lights*. Portland, OR: Alaska Northwest Books.

Evans, R. (2002). *The light of Christmas*. New York: Simon & Schuster.

Fleischmann, P. (1999). *Weslandia*. Cambridge, MA: Candlewick.

Fleischman, P., & Frampton, D. (1995). *Bull Run*. New York: HarperCollins.

Fletcher, R. (2003). *Hello, harvest moon*. New York: Clarion.

Fletcher, R. (1997). *Twilight comes twice*. New York: Clarion.

Fox, M. (1989). *Feathers and fools*. New York: Harcourt.

Frank, J. (2004). *The toughest cowboy: Or how the West was tamed*. New York, NY: Simon & Schuster.

Fuchs, B. (2004). *Ride like the wind: A tale of the Pony Express*. New York: Blue Sky Press.

Galan, M. (1997). *There's still time: The success of the endangered species act*. Washington, D.C.: National Geographic Society.

Garland, S. (2004). *The lotus seed*. New York: Scholastic.

Gibbons, G. (1993). *Spiders*. New York: Holiday House.

Giovanni, N. (2005). *Rosa*. New York: Henry Holt.

Gonsalves, R., & Thomson, S. L. (2003). *Imagine a night*. New York: Simon & Schuster.

Grifalconi, A. (1986). *The village of round and square houses*. New York: Little, Brown.

Helldorfer, M. C. (2000). *Hog music*. New York: Penguin.

Henkes, K. (2000). *Wemberly worried*. Cambridge, MA: Greenwillow.

Hest, A. (1997). *When Jessie came across the sea*. Cambridge, MA: Candlewick.

Howard, E. F. (2000). *Virgie goes to school with us boys*. New York: Simon & Schuster.

Isaacs, A. (1994). *Swamp angel*. New York: Dutton.

Johnson, J. (2006). *Rain forest*. New York: Houghton Mifflin.

LaMarche, J. (2000). *The raft*. New York: HarperCollins.

Lawlor, L. (2002). *Old Crump: The true story of a trip west*. New York: Holiday House.

Lewis, E. B. (2005). *This little light of mine*. New York: Simon & Schuster.

Lewis, P. O. (1999). *Storm boy*. Berkeley, CA: Tricycle Press.

Lewis, P. O. (1997). *Frog girl*. Berkeley, CA: Tricycle Press.

London, J., & London, A. (2001). *White water*. New York: Penguin Putnam.

Long, L., & Ogburn, J. (2003). *The lady and the lion: A brothers Grimm tale (A retelling)*. New York: Dial.

Longfellow, H., & Bing, C. (2001). *The midnight ride of Paul Revere*. Brooklyn, NY: Handprint Books.

Longfellow, H. W., & Rand, T. (1990). *Paul Revere's ride*. New York: Penguin Group.

Locker, T. (1997). *Mountain dance*. New York: Harcourt.

Locker, T. (1997). *Water dance*. New York: Harcourt.

Locker, T., & Edgar, M.D. (2003). *John Muir: America's naturalist*. Golden, CO: Fulcrum Publishing.

Lorbiecki, M. (1998). *Sister Anne's hands*. New York: Dial.

Lumry, A., & Hurwitz, L.(2003). *Adventures of Riley: Tigers in Terai*. Bellevue, WA: Eaglemont Press.

Lyon, G. E. (2003). *Mother to tigers*. New York: Atheneum.

MacLachlan, P. (1985). *Sarah, plain and tall*. New York: HarperCollins.

Marshall, J. (1997). *George and Martha*. New York: Houghton Mifflin.

Martin, B., & Archambault, J. (1987). *Knots on a counting rope*. New York: Henry Holt.

McBrier, P. (2001). *Beatrice's goat*. New York: Aladdin.

Medearis, A. S., & Shaffer, T. (1994). *The singing man: Adapted from a West African folktale*. New York: Holiday House.

Melmed, L. K. (1997). *Little Oh*. New York: HarperCollins.

Miller, D. S. (1997) *Disappearing lake: Nature's magic in Denali National Park*. New York: Walker & Company.

Mills, L. (1991). *The Rag Coat*. New York: Little, Brown.

Musgrove, M. (1977). *Ashanti to Zulu: African traditions*. New York: Dial.

Musgrove, M., & Cairns, J. (2001). *The spider weaver: A legend of kente cloth*. New York: Blue Sky Press.

Nelson, V. N. (2003). *Almost to freedom*. New York: Scholastic.

Noble, T. H. (2004). *The scarlet stockings spy*. Chelsea, MI: Sleeping Bear Press.

Ogburn, J. K., & Long, L. (2000). *The magic nesting doll*. New York: Dial.

Onyefulu, I. (1993). *A is for Africa*. New York: Dutton.

Paulsen, G. (1999). *Canoe days*. New York: Dragonfly.

Paulsen, G. (1995). *Dogteam*. New York: Dragonfly.

Park, F., & Park, G. (2000). *The royal bee*. Honesdale, PA: Boyds Mills Press.

Pilkey, D. (2003). *Kat Kong*. New York: Harcourt.

Pinkney, A.D. (1999) *Bill Pickett: Rodeo-ridin' cowboy.* New York: Voyager.

Prelutsky, J. (1984). *It's snowing! It's snowing!* New York: Greenwillow.

Rappaport, D. (2001). *Martin's big words: The life of Dr. Martin Luther King, Jr.* New York: Hyperion.

Ryder, J. (2001). *The waterfall's gift.* San Francisco: The Sierra Club.

San Souci, R. (1989). *The talking eggs.* New York: Dial.

San Souci, R., & Walsh, R. (2004). *The well at the end of the world.* San Francisco: Chronicle Books.

Sanderson, R. (2004). *The snow princess.* New York: Little, Brown.

Schaefer, L., & Swiatkowska, G. (2004). *Arrowhawk.* New York: Henry Holt.

Schroeder, A., & Pinkney, J. (1996). *Minty: A story of young Harriet Tubman.* New York: Puffin.

Shasha, M. (2002). *Night of the moonjellies.* Keller, TX: Purple House Press.

Sloat, T., & Sloat, R. (1993). *The hungry giant of the tundra. (A retelling)* Portland, OR: Alaska Northwest Books.

Smith, M., & Smith, R.(2004). *E Is for evergreen: A Washington alphabet.* Chelsea, MI: Sleeping Bear Press.

Spinelli, E. (2004). *Feathers: Poems about birds.* New York: Henry Holt.

Stainton, S. (2007). *Santa's snow cat (reprint).* New York: HarperTrophy.

Steptoe, J. (1987). *Mufaro's beautiful daughters.* New York: HarperTrophy.

Stewart, S. (2007). *The gardener.* New York: Square Fish.

Stock, C. (1993). *Where are you going, Manyoni?* New York: HarperCollins.

Trottier, M. (2003). *The paint box.* Ontario, Canada: Fitzhenry & Whiteside.

Van Allsburg, C. (2006). *Probuditi!* New York: Houghton Mifflin.

Van Allsburg, C. (1993). *The sweetest fig.* New York: Houghton Mifflin.

Van Allsburg, C. (1992). *The widow's broom.* New York: Houghton Mifflin Company.

Van Allsburg, C. (1988). *Two bad ants.* New York: Houghton Mifflin.

Van Allsburg, C. (1984). *The mysteries of Harris Burdick.* New York: Houghton Mifflin.

Van Allsburg, C. (1981). *Jumanji.* New York: Houghton Mifflin.

Van Allsburg, C. (1979). *The garden of Abdul Gasazi.* New York: Houghton Mifflin.

Vaughan, R. L. & Christiansen, L. (2000). *Eagle Boy: A Pacific Northwest native tale.* Seattle, WA: Sasquatch Books.

Venezia, M. (1988). Getting to know the world's greatest artists series: *Van Gogh.* Children's Press.

Weatherford, C. (2006). *Moses: When Harriet Tubman led her people to freedom.* New York: Hyperion.

Wiesner, D. (1995). *June 29, 1999.* New York: Clarion Books.

Winstead, A. (2003). *The star spangled banner.* Nashville, TN: Ideals Publications.

Wood, D. (1996). *Northwoods cradle song: From a Menominee lullaby.* New York: Simon & Schuster.

Woodson, J. (2004). *Coming on home soon.* New York: Putnam.

Woodson, J. (2001). *The other side.* New York: Putnam.

Wright, B. (2005). *The blizzard.* New York: Holiday House.

Yep, L. & Mak, K. (1997). *The dragon prince: A Chinese beauty and the beast tale.* HarperCollins.

Yolen, J. (1992). *Encounter.* New York: Harcourt.

Yolen, J. (1991). *Greyling.* New York: Philomel.

Yolen, J., & Semple, J. (2000). *Color me a rhyme: Nature poems for young people.* Honesdale, PA: Wordsong/Boyds Mills Press.

Young, E. (1989). *Lon Po Po: A Red-riding Hood story from China.* New York: Philomel.

Professional Works Cited

Allington, R. (2005). *What really matters for struggling readers: Designing research based programs* (2nd ed.). Boston: Allyn & Bacon.

Beers, K. (2002). *When kids can't read: What teachers can do: A guide for teachers 6-12.* Portsmouth, NH: Heinemann.

Burke, J. English Companion. Retrieved March 10, 2008, from http://www.englishcompanion.com.

Cigrand, M., & Howard, P. (2000). *Easy literature-based quilt around the year.* New York: Scholastic.

Durkin, D. (1978). What classroom observations reveal about reading instruction. *Reading Research Quarterly,* 14, pp. 481–533.

Fountas, I. C., & Pinnell, G. (2001). *Guiding readers and writers grades 3-6: Teaching comprehension, genre, and content literacy.* Portsmouth, NH: Heinemann.

Harvey, S., & Goudvis, A. (2007). *Strategies that work: Teaching comprehension to enhance understanding* (2nd ed.) York, ME: Stenhouse.

Harwayne, S. (2000). *Lifetime guarantees.* Portsmouth, NH: Heinemann.

Hoyt, L. (2002). *Make it real: Strategies for success with informational text.* Portsmouth, NH: Heinemann.

Hoyt, L. (1998). *Revisit, reflect, retell: Strategies for improving reading comprehension.* Portsmouth, NH: Heinemann.

Keene, E., & Zimmermann, S. (2007). *Mosaic of Thought: The power of comprehension instruction.* (2nd ed.) Portsmouth, NH: Heinemann.

Marzano, R. J., Pickering, D. J., & Pollock, J. E. (2001). *Classroom instruction that works: Research based strategies for increasing student achievement.* Englewood Cliffs, NJ: Prentice Hall.

Miller, D. (2002). *Reading with meaning: Teaching comprehension in the primary grades.* York, ME: Stenhouse.

Pearson, P. D., & L. Fielding. (1991). Comprehension instruction. In M. Kamil, P. Mosenthal, P.D. Pearson, R. Barr (Eds.). *Handbook of reading research, Vol II:* 815–860. NY: Longman.

Pressley, M. (2006). *Reading instruction that works: The case for balanced teaching* (3rd ed.). New York, NY: Guilford Press.

Pressley, M. (2006, Apr. 29). What the future of reading research could be. Paper presented to The International Reading Association. Chicago, Illinois.

Rabinowitz, P. J. (1997). *Before reading: Narrative connections and the politics of interpretation.* Columbus: Ohio State University Press.

Serafini, F. (2004). *Lessons in comprehension: Explicit instruction in the reading workshop.* Portsmouth, NH: Heinemann.

Serafini, F. & Serafini-Youngs, S. (2006). *Around the reading workshop in 180 Days: A month-by-month guide to effective instruction.* Portsmouth, NH: Heinemann.